JOHN HOWARD FROM THE PAVILION

SHAPING THE ASCENT TO POWER

EDITOR ANDREW BLYTH | FOREWORD PAUL KELLY

Published in 2023 by Connor Court Publishing Pty Ltd.

The articles in this volume are reproduced with permission of *The Australian.*

Connor Court Publishing Pty Ltd
PO Box 7257
Redland Bay QLD 4165
sales@connorcourt.com
www.connorcourt.com

ISBN: 9781922815392

Cover design by Ian James

Cover photo: UNSW Canberra John Howard Prime Ministerial Library

Printed in Australia

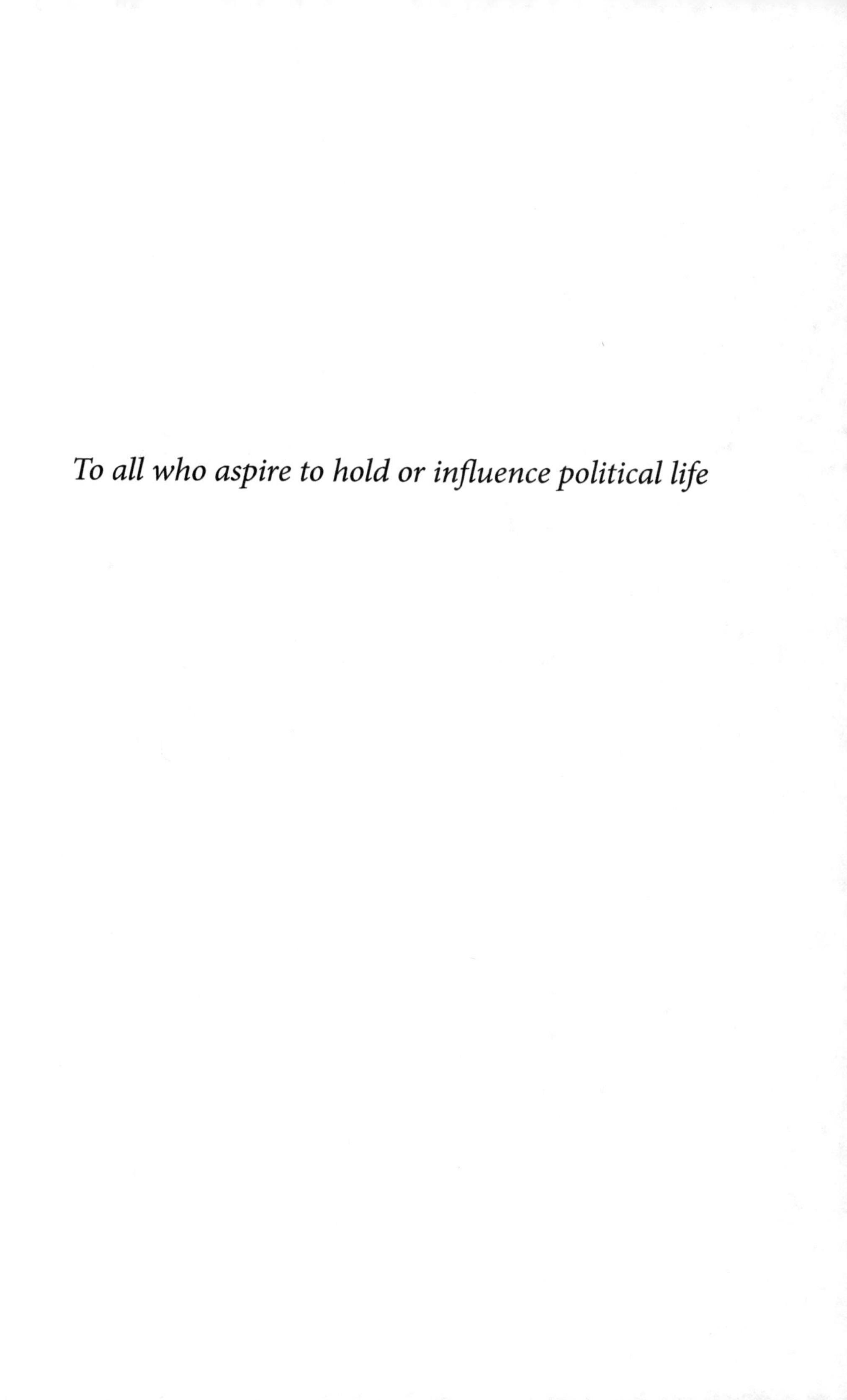

To all who aspire to hold or influence political life

CONTENTS

Articles

June 1989

July 1989

August 1989

ACRONYMS

A$ - Australian Dollar

ABC – Australian Broadcasting Corporation

ACT – Australian Capital Territory

ACTU – Australian Council of Trade Unions

AIDS – acquired immunodeficiency syndrome

ALP – Australian Labor Party

AMSWU - Amalgamated Metal Workers and Shipwrights Union

ANC – African National Congress

ANZUS – Australia New Zealand United States Treaty

BHP – Broken Hill Proprietary Company

EPAC - Economic Planning Advisory Council

G7 – Group of Seven

GDP – Gross Domestic Product

ICAC – Independent Commission Against Corruption

IMF – International Monetary Fund

INF – Intermediate-Range Nuclear Forces Treaty

LDP – Liberal Democratic Party

MX – Missile, Experimental

NATO – North Atlantic Treaty Organization

OECD – Organisation for Economic Cooperation and Development

TNT – Thomas Nationwide Transport

UK – United Kingdom

USSR – Union of Soviet Socialist Republics

US – United States of America

VFL – Victorian Football League

Acknowledgements

This book has been made possible through the generosity of Australia's 25th and second-longest serving prime minister, The Honourable John Howard OM, AC and my colleagues at the University of New South Wales Canberra John Howard Prime Ministerial Library and Exhibition located at Old Parliament House: Professor Brenton Prosser, Annette Carter, and Trish Burgess. I thank the friendly and helpful staff of the UNSW Canberra Library and UNSW Special Collections team based at the Australian Defence Force Academy as well as the ever-patient staff of the National Library of Australia. I am also grateful to Emeritus Professor David Lovell, immediate past director of the Howard Library for his enthusiasm and goodwill. None of this of course would have been possible were it not for the vision and drive of my good friend and mentor, Professor Tom Frame AM, inaugural director of the Howard Library.

Over the last seven years it has been a privilege to act as a custodian of the private collection of papers held at the John Howard Prime Ministerial Library and Exhibition located at Old Parliament House. Opened officially on December 4, 2018, the 'Howard Library' holds some 10,000 items of personal papers, official records, political memorabilia, photographs and documents from John Howard's political career, dating from 1974 to 2007. Through the support of the Commonwealth Government, the University of New South Wales Canberra, private donors and sponsors, visitors can connect with the life and career of John Howard and are introduced to the contest of ideas through key debates during the Howard Government.

The United States makes much of the history of their presidents – with museums and research centres for every president. Australia, disappointingly, takes an ad-hoc approach to prime ministerial libraries. While there are libraries and institutes for John Curtin, Robert Menzies, Gough Whitlam, Bob Hawke and John Howard, we need more of them. They are an invaluable time capsule of political history at a time of declining trust in government. As political biographer, Sir Anthony Seldon argues, 'an understanding and respect for the past makes for better decisions and for better people'. Seldon is spot on.

This book illustrates the importance John Howard placed on articulating his views and participating in the contest of ideas. There is much to be said of his discipline in penning a weekly column and how current (and future) public leaders can learn from him.

Foreword

Paul Kelly, Editor At Large, *The Australian*

In May 1989 John Howard was deposed as leader of the Liberal Party in a move that was widely assumed to have terminated his prospects of becoming prime minister. Andrew Peacock beat Howard by the convincing margin of 44 to 27 votes and the Liberals embraced a new team with Peacock as leader and Fred Chaney as his deputy. The well planned and ruthlessly executed challenge had taken Howard by surprise.

He admitted to being 'devastated.' Asked at a press conference about his prospects of returning as leader, Howard famously replied 'like Lazarus with a triple bypass.' His closest colleagues saw the event as the turning point in his career. Howard said later: 'I felt that it was the end of my dream to be PM.'

The history of these events is long forgotten but the Peacock backers wanted Howard out. In the end Peacock offered him the shadow education portfolio, a none too subtle snub to a man who had been 14 years a frontbencher, five as treasurer and five as leader. Howard said he would take defence; Peacock refused. Howard went to the backbench. He was bruised but not finished.

Within days the Peacock transition was engulfed in ugly recriminations. The key organisers of the challenge appeared in an ABC *Four Corners* program describing the secrecy, lying and manipulation behind their successful challenge. This triggered a groundswell of support for Howard and federal director, Tony Eggleton, said grass roots party sentiment was 'as strong a reaction' as anything he had seen in his 15 years as director. Howard's immediate fate was as a high-profile backbencher as the party struggled under Peacock to mount a tenable campaign at the 1990 election against Bob Hawke, an election Peacock lost.

As National Affairs Editor at *The Australian* covering these events, I believed the 1989 leadership challenge was a mistake. My view was reinforced by the ineptitude the Peacock camp showed towards Howard with the internal rupture undermining Peacock as a returned leader.

During talks with Howard at this time we canvassed the option of him writing columns for The Australian. I knew that Howard had always been interested in journalism and that he would need a voice from the backbench. As a result, I spoke to the late Frank Devine, editor of the paper. Frank was an immediate enthusiast and sealed the deal with Howard. Over six months he wrote 23 columns. They served as a form of therapy for Howard who said he 'loved' writing them.

The columns attracted a wider and positive response. Context was the key. Howard wrote with clarity and opened the lens wide. He wrote about politics, domestic policy, political principles and foreign affairs. But what mattered was the way he wrote – it was muscular and frank. These columns offer a remarkable insight into what Howard really thought during 1989, a critical year in world history. Some of his judgments were prescient, others less so. Howard understood that you don't write a column without something to say.

As a backbencher he was not constrained to just echo Liberal policy under Peacock. Howard defended his own policies and offered many personal and original reflections on both Australia and the state of the world. But the unifying theme is Howard's sense of policy conviction. On display are many of the issues and policies that he would later pursue as prime minister.

One column that won conspicuous attention was devoted to Australia's cricket captain, Allan Border, with Howard seeing in

Border true sportsmanship based on 'winning and grace.' Re-reading that column it is tempting to think Howard saw parallels between himself and Border as he described the cricket captain as someone who has 'gone through the rough times, tasted defeat, faced up to the pressure and displayed great resilience.'

The article was more about character than cricket with Howard saying Border's behaviour showed that 'violent personal hatred and vitriol' towards opponents was not necessary to sporting success. He quoted Sir Donald Bradman's assessment that in considering an athlete's stature he set store by dignity, integrity, courage and, 'perhaps most of all' modesty. Border had shown these qualities.

Howard wrote at a time of high current account deficit, damaging inflation and high foreign debt off the back of the 1980s boom – the response of the Reserve Bank and the government being rising interest rates to stabilise the economy. But the interest rate crunch in the new world of a de-regulated economy would finish in a deep recession the following year.

In his columns Howard made sustained arguments for more micro-economic reform, the need to de-regulate the labour market, push the privatization agenda, reform the waterfront, boost productivity and address the damaging impact of high marginal rates on personal income taxpayers. He advanced a strong agenda, not necessarily popular, but a coherent framework for more market-based reform.

His approach was not to criticise Bob Hawke and Paul Keating for their pro-market reforms but urge them to go further, 'to finish the de-regulatory job.' The difference from the politics of the last decade in Australia could hardly be greater.

Unsurprisingly, Howard warned the interest rate strategy ran the risk of 'overkill' and squeezing too much life out of the economy. But his most sustained theme was the labour market, the need to end the 'privileged' legal position of the trade unions, terminate the centralised system whose existence depended upon union power and move to a model where wages were set in negotiations between employers and employees.

Howard dealt with the pilots' dispute in several columns. He wanted the dispute resolved in a settlement between the pilots and the airlines – and felt his position was 'closer to the real effect of Hawke's strategy than Andrew Peacock's.' With Hawke running a fierce campaign against the Pilots Federation Howard, in essence, urged a market-based outcome hoping the dispute would lead to a more de-regulated system.

With a Queensland state election looming and memories of the 'Joh for Canberra' campaign Howard offered the view that 'the Nationals warrant a spell on the sidelines.' He said the Queensland party needs to clean up its act. His advice was that Liberals were right to reject the 'junior role' in any coalition while Howard made it clear he was not supporting Labor - but it was academic since Labor would win the election.

It was a time of epic global change. Howard welcomed the historic reforms of Mikhail Gorbachev but said his purpose was to save the communist system not convert to liberal democracy. With the revolutions unfolding in Eastern Europe, Howard called for big ideas and major investments to help the new capitalist democracies. It was time to 'act boldly.'

The most important column was his last on 3 November 1989. Howard said: 'No decade in my lifetime has ended on a more optimistic note than the 1980s. Politically there is more cause for genuine hope amongst the nations of the world than probably at any time since the end of the World War II.' The decade was ending with the victory of capitalism and free enterprise over collectivism. He nominated Paul Volker the 'economic hero' of the 1980s for re-imposing monetary discipline in the teeth of opposition and laying the basis for economic expansion.

Howard welcomed the floating of the Australian dollar, the end of our economic insularity and the improved quality of the economic debate in public life. 'The 1980s was the era of financial market deregulation,' Howard wrote. 'The 1990s must be the era of labour market deregulation.' To an extent his prediction was verified in a way he didn't envisage at the time of writing – with Howard as PM.

His columns came to an end when Peacock offered Howard a frontbench position as spokesman on manufacturing industry. Howard said he 'didn't particularly enjoy' returning to the frontbench but knew it was the right decision. He said he found writing 'immensely satisfying.' The country had lost a columnist; it would gain a prime minister.

Appreciation

Miranda Devine

The week before my father Frank Devine died, John Howard visited him at the hospice and pepped him up with one of his favourite things: gossip!

The two men were so easy in each other's company, even in such an intimate setting, that you would think they were old friends. And, in fact, I think they were, rare as genuine friendships are between a journalist and a politician, who each want something from the other that the other doesn't want to give.

But the Devine-Howard affection began simply in 1989 as a mutual adventure in journalism. The future prime minister was a newly deposed opposition leader brooding over his future on the back bench and my father, then the editor-in-chief of the Australian, hired him to write a weekly column for the princely sum of $800 a pop.

'This is a pretty exciting undertaking, I think,' wrote my father in an encouraging letter to Howard on May 19, 1989, confirming the arrangement and offering useful tips on column writing.

'Winston Churchill and Jack Kennedy (and Eleanor Roosevelt!) come to mind especially as persons of affairs who were genuinely distinguished as journalists.'

It was a new lease of life for a bruised backbencher looking down the barrel of his 50th birthday, and whose political prospects during that time were best summed up by the brutal *Bulletin* cover: 'Mr 18 per cent. Why on earth does this man bother?'

The columns were a hit with readers and the editor was delighted by his protégé's uncommon writing talent. Over the six short months of this serendipitous arrangement, the two men cemented what would be a lifelong mutual admiration. While quite different in personality, they both were natural enthusiasts and shared a passion for cricket. I'm not sure if Howard had bookcases full of old Wisdens that he used to dog-ear in the bath, but his erudition on googlies and golden ducks delighted my father.

Howard's budding journalistic career was cut short when he was drafted back onto the front bench at the end of the year and my father had to sack him immediately. As Howard's political ascent accelerated, his former editor took pride in having played a small part by showcasing his ideas at *The Australian* during that brief wilderness period.

My father ever after would marvel at what a good and clear writer he was, the ultimate compliment from one journalist to another, and, of course, after his phenomenal innings as a four-term prime minister, Howard resumed his second career as an author, writing the best-selling political memoir in Australian history, *Lazarus Rising*. He followed up four years later with an acclaimed 720-page biography of Robert Menzies, the only prime minister to have served longer in office. The columns in this book foreshadowed these literary triumphs, the vindication of my father's early faith.

Towards the end of Howard's last term in office my father likened him to the similarly plain-spoken and underestimated American wartime president Harry Truman. 'Charisma is not part of John Howard's political equipment,' he wrote in 2005. 'But for a decade [Australian voters] have stayed faithful to a man who is clearly one of them and, almost paradoxically, a decisive leader with a record of right choices.' Beyond cricket and columns, I think the two men remained friends because they appreciated each other's innate decency.

Howard never cashed in on his prime ministership in retirement, or sniped at his successors through the media, or gratuitously inserted himself into the political fray. He never suffered from relevance deprivation syndrome because he had another talent besides politics, as you will see in these pages.

Preface

This book is a reproduction of John Howard's weekly columns published in the national broadsheet, *The Australian* in 1989. His articles are a time capsule of evolving national and world events as the sun set on the 1980s. Presenting readers with a variety of topical issues, Howard's columns are laced with political insights and anecdotes revealing his craft for engaging commentary. Offering readers a window into his beliefs and drive for political reform, Howard delves into economic uncertainty caused by high interest rates, increasing national debt, and rising unemployment as well as assessments on unfolding events in Eastern Europe, apartheid in South Africa, unrest in China, and the rise of Japan. We are also reminded of his passion for sport, namely cricket and his admiration for Australian Test Cricket captain, Allan Border. Howard moves seamlessly across economic, political and social affairs with enthusiasm and composure offering policy prescriptions that he as 'Lazarus with a triple bypass' would later adopt in shaping the ascent to power on 2 March 1996.

LEADER OF THE OPPOSITION

After a failed attempt as opposition leader to topple Bob Hawke's Labor government in the 1987 election, Howard's popularity dipped so low that the now-defunct Bulletin magazine ran a cover picture of him tagged: "Mr 18 per cent. Why on earth does this man bother?" When deposed by his bitter rival Andrew Peacock, Howard remarked ruefully that in order to resurrect his leadership he would have to be "Lazarus with a triple bypass".

Source: UNSW Canberra John Howard Prime Ministerial Library website: www.howardlibrary.unsw.edu.au

Prologue

The now defunct *The Bulletin* magazine published on 20 December 1988, portrays an image on its cover of a stoic John Howard alongside a headline crying out, 'Mr. 18%: Why on earth does this man bother?'. The Morgan Gallup poll reveals Howard's approval rating for 'better prime minister' at 18 per cent compared with Bob Hawke's commanding lead of 69 per cent. Hawke was proving himself a popular prime minister, having won re-election in 1984 (seeing off his Liberal challenger, Andrew Peacock), driving ambitious economic and social reform, and leading bicentenary celebrations earlier in the year. Hawke had an impenetrable lead.

In defiance, John Howard continued to develop policies, meet community leaders, deliver speeches, and take the fight up to the Hawke Government in Parliament. Howard's efforts were not to be rewarded. Having succeeded Peacock as Liberal leader in 1985 and having lost the 1987 federal election – in part because of Coalition disunity created by the notorious 'Joh for Canberra' push – a small but determined cohort of Howard's colleagues believed his time was up. They organised against him. A political operator as sharp and attuned as Howard was caught by surprise.

Tuesday 9 May 1989 was a tumultuous day in John Howard's political career. He was politically executed as Leader of the Liberal Party by rogue elements within the Party room. Working in secret, a core group of members had assiduously cultivated enough votes over many months to force a leadership spill. Howard was caught off-guard. Supporters of Andrew Peacock secured their man the top job. Winning at all costs had spread to the Federal Liberal Party. Howard was rocked to his core.

His parliamentary colleagues, John Moore MP, Wilson Tuckey MP, Chris Puplick MP, David Jull MP, and Peter Shack MP were later to reveal their treachery in an ABC Television *Four Corners* program (aired in August), titled 'True Believer – 1989'. The group of five were writ large boasting of their plotting and scheming. Howard described the surprise leadership coup as 'an act without honour' and the prospects of him resurrecting his leadership in the future as akin to 'Lazarus with a triple bypass'.

Faced with the choice of remaining as the Member for Bennelong (elected in 1974) or returning to the law, Howard turned to his family and friends for counsel. He was to be 50 in July, young enough to make a career as a lawyer and provide for his family. After much reflection, and time spent away from the political fray, Howard chose to stay and fight for the beliefs he valued.

An active participant in the contest of ideas, Howard set about writing a weekly column for *The Australian,* from June to November 1989. No topic was spared. Howard penned over two dozen articles ranging from the economy, industrial relations, foreign affairs, to sport, drugs and organised crime. His articles were candid, engaging and topical. His anecdotes resonated with readers. Regarded as 'one of our calmest and most thoughtful political leaders', Howard relished the chance to share his views with a wider audience free of political constraints. He was to publish his twenty-third and valedictory column ahead of his return to the shadow Cabinet.

Howard's time in the political wilderness allowed him to reflect and refine his political beliefs (much like Menzies) and position himself to return as Leader of the Federal Liberal Party in January 1995. Howard would secure a record majority of seats at the next federal election and go on to become Australia's 25th and second-longest serving prime minister, from March 1996 to November 2007. His published articles are reproduced in this book.

Andrew Blyth
Editor
May 2023

JUNE 1989

Friday, 2 June 1989, p. 13

1

Drawing on his experience as former Treasurer and Leader of the Opposition, Howard, in his first article tackles the Hawke Government's penchant of shooting the messenger. US bond credit rating business Moody's and credit rating agency Standard and Poor's are in the firing line for doing their job. With economic problems of our own making, Howard outlines an uncomplicated strategy of increasing national productivity and national savings to deliver a more efficient and competitive economy.

'A disturbing case of messenger's disease'

The bodies of slain messengers are beginning to pile high on Australia's economic battle ground.

This is hardly surprising – slaying the messenger has been an age-old response of people and societies who do not want to hear bad news and who pretend that things are other than what they really are.

The latest body is that of Moody's rating service – executed for having had the temerity merely to admit to doing its job.

It is hard to imagine what a rating agency is supposed to do other than periodically review ratings and produce the conclusions of those reviews.

Whether Moody's enjoys some resurrection if its conclusions square with those of Standard and Poor's – which has not marked Australia down – remains to be seen.

The Moody's issue will fade. Two other examples of attacking the messenger with much greater long-term implications for sensible economic debate in Australia, will not.

They are the growing rumblings of discontent about foreign investment and blaming banks for high interest rates.

Foreign investors and bankers are currently attracting growing attention because they convey and symbolise some unpalatable facts of economic life.

Opposition to foreign investment has no rational basis. It is highly emotional. More ominously it manifests the frustration of people who know they are losing control over their own future.

In hitting foreign investment, they are choosing the wrong target. Our huge dependence on foreign money is only a symptom of our economic problem and not the problem itself.

We would be in even greater trouble if foreign money were not flowing in at the present rate.

The nature of that foreign money is important.

If it is invested in solid assets, it will stay here and help in the development of our nation.

If it is simply hot money in search of high interest rates it can flow out just as quickly with disastrous effects.

So if Australia were now to restrict foreign investment we would simply be deciding to cut our living standards even further.

As both sides of politics acknowledge, we now spend far more than we produce. The difference is made up by imports.

While we continue down this path, we must draw on the savings of foreigners to buy those imports as we don't have enough savings of our own.

There are two ways of solving the problem. We can reduce our spending (which means cutting our standard of living) or we can increase our output.

In the short term some reduction in spending is unavoidable.

In the longer term our choice must be to concentrate on lifting national productivity.

Unless we do we have no hope of permanently closing the gap

between our exports and imports. Any other response side-steps the real problem.

'Joining a lynch-mob chorus against foreign investors won't lower interest rates'

Only such a response will make our export and import competing industries more competitive. Other ploys are temporary palliatives.

The government has chosen to choke off import demand by imposing higher interest rates on the private sector. Eventually that will close the gap but the cost in recessionary terms could be quite horrendous.

As the government has no comprehensive productivity strategy then interest rate attrition is in the short term the only alternative. But it really does miss the main problem.

Instead of pointless speculation about how soon high interest rates will slow demand, and whether the landing will be hard, soft, medium or bone-crunching, we should adopt measures which permanently deliver a more efficient and competitive economy.

That is why policy debate about higher levels of national productivity, national savings and the jargonistically called 'micro-economic reform agenda' is so important.

Incidentally, we should try to find a better term than 'micro-economic reforms'. We should start talking instead about a more efficient economy.

That, after all, is what lifting productivity is all about. It is about using our physical, human and financial resources more efficiently. It involves dismantling restrictive work practices. It also demands the political courage on both sides to deregulate one's own constituencies.

It is always so easy to call for the other fellow to inflict the pain of structural adjustment on those more disposed to support his point of view.

That is why the wheat decision was so important for the coalition. That is why we all await with interest the government's waterfront and coastal shipping reforms. They are a real test of political courage in dealing with constituencies very close to home.

There is emotional resentment towards foreign investment – particularly the rise in Japanese investment.

However, one thing is crystal clear. Although there may be some short-term political mileage in either appearing to or actually taking a tougher line on foreign investment in straight national interest terms, it is illogical short-sighted and worst of all, diverts public gaze from the real problem.

If we worry about a few percentage points increase in foreign ownership of real estate, we postpone other decisions so essential to make our economy more efficient.

We will make foreign investment the scapegoat. In the process we will miss the obvious point that rising dependence on foreign money is not only unavoidable but conveys a sharp painful signal about frailties in our own economy.

Today's vocal opponents of foreign investment – wherever they sit in the political spectrum – also ignore economic history both of Australia and other nations.

They ignore the historic contribution of foreign investment to the development of the United States' economy in the 19th century. They also ignore the enormous benefits of foreign investment to the development of our resources sector in the post-war period.

A similar case of shooting the messenger is the latter-day attempt by some, including senior government ministers, to blame high interest rates on the banks.

I hold no brief for Australian banks or indeed any financial institution.

Moreover, I believe the major banks have thus far done a poor job of properly explaining the cause of high interest rates, particularly at a time when banks are enjoying seemingly high profit levels.

The banks have a public relations challenge to rebut the perception eagerly fostered by the government, traditional opponents of banks and some media that it is the avarice of our major lenders and not policy follies which are the cause of middle Australia's monthly interest rate strangulation.

That having been said, our gigantic foreign debt, the need to service an ever-increasing current account deficit and above average inflation rates all condemn Australia to a high interest rate structure indefinitely.

Australian banks are as much the captives of this as anyone else. They are easy political pickings because it is they who deal with the public and pass on the bad news to borrowers.

Those politicians and others who flay them know this only too well.

When the Reserve Bank tightens monetary policy, thus jacking up home mortgage rates, it is not the urbane Governor of the Reserve Bank, Mr Johnstone[1], who sends out the letters to Australian home buyers advising of interest rate adjustments.

Rather they are sent by our increasingly unpopular bank managers.

Yet no serious observer of the Australian economy can fairly dispute that it is the determination of the government in concert with the Reserve Bank to keep a tight monetary policy which has pushed up interest rates.

As the Governor of the Reserve Bank himself said on 17 May 1989,

> 'In the strategy of restraint tight monetary policy has and undoubtedly will continue to have a major role. Although it

[1] Governor of the Reserve Bank of Australia, August 1982 – July 1989.

is a blunt instrument it is an effective one. Tight monetary policy means high interest rates.'

Some simple realities should be kept in mind. One of those is that banks actually make higher profits as interest rates fall. Another more important reality is that there are savers as well as borrowers. Banks must pay for their funds. They get no funds if they don't pay decent rates. Middle class savers are a lot smarter than they used to be. They shop around for a good bargain.

It should also be noted that as an industry the rate of return on shareholders' funds from banks is about average. In 1988 it was the ninth highest out of 23 industry groups.

Banks have obligations to shareholders as well as customers. In many cases they are the same people.

As huge institutions they have social obligations as well.

In today's economic climate Australian banks are not only major players in their own right, but they carry direct signals and messages to their customers about economic conditions.

For borrowers those messages are at present very unpalatable.

Just as the slaughter of messengers in ancient times did not win more battles, verbally or otherwise disposing of your bank manager or joining a lynch-mob chorus against foreign investors won't lower interest rates or reduce our national debt.

*****

Friday, 9 June 1989, p. 13

2

The democratic push by students challenging the authority of the Chinese Communist party resulted in carnage in Beijing's Tiananmen Square has Howard questioning whether a similar response is likely in Moscow's Red Square.

'To see or hear no evil is to lose the war of ideology'

In August 1980, as Treasurer in the Fraser Government, I instructed the Australian representative on the Interim Committee of the International Monetary Fund to vote against an attempt then underway to effectively steal from Taiwan her gold deposits with the Fund and credit those deposits to the People's Republic of China.

China had been a foundation member of the Fund in 1945. By 1980 it had long since been accepted that the Beijing Government represented the people of China.

However, the gold deposits were another matter. Although there had been some gold lodged with the Fund prior to 1949 the great bulk had accumulated from deposits made by the Taiwanese after the Communist take-over.

To have supported the Beijing Government's case in 1980 would have been to have sanctioned an act of international financial brigandry. Fortunately, the attempt narrowly failed despite a strong push from many European and Third World countries.

There was also a lot of support in many sections of the Australian bureaucracy – but not including The Treasury.

I recalled this incident as I read, saw and heard of the carnage in Tiananmen Square earlier this week.

The point of the Taiwan gold story is that despite its blatant injustice the proposal attracted immense support and almost succeeded.

It was a sample of the strong mood throughout the West from the early 1970s onwards to neither see nor hear any evil so far as the People's Republic was concerned.

This is not 'I told you so' hindsight criticism. Commonsense demanded that the isolation of China end. Richard Nixon's[2] greatest foreign policy achievement was to open a dialogue with China.

Successive Australian governments of both persuasions deserve credit for having attempted to build a relationship with the Chinese people. Those attempts should go on.

Likewise, it would be foolish for the West – including Australia – to rush to impose economic sanctions, or the like in retaliation for what has now happened in China.

That we should be repelled and shocked by the brutality is quite understandable. Whether we should be surprised at the turn of events, as distinct from the natural revulsion at such a human tragedy, is another matter.

It goes to the heart of the west's proper understanding of a totalitarian state.

The student democratic push in China challenged the fundamental authority of the Communist party. That is why it was brutally put down.

Despite the apparently greater political changes which have occurred in the Soviet Union, a similar assault on the basic grip of the Communist party in the USSR could bring a like response.

We should not imagine that what happened in Tiananmen Square could not also happen in Red Square.

If that is thought extreme, be reminded that the Tiananmen Square blood bath was ordered by the most liberal regime Communist China has seen.

---

[2] Richard Nixon, 37th President of the United States, January 20, 1969 – August 9, 1974.

Also have a careful look at the way in which the Soviet authorities have dealt with ethnic and regional unrest in various parts of the USSR.

There are parallels now in attitude to Gorbachev's Russia to the attitudes held towards China in the late 1970s and 80s.

'That we should be repelled is understandable. Whether we should be surprised...'

Ideological criticism or even reservations about the Soviet Union these days are derided by most media and many politicians, who should know better, as backward-looking cold war rhetoric.

John Spender, the former Shadow Foreign Minister copped just such a blast when he released the Coalition's foreign policy early in April.

That document is the most lucid recital of foreign policy that the Liberal Party has released for some years. It squarely faces the realities and challenges of the modern world.

It welcomed the positive steps under Gorbachev but cautioned against going overboard.

Quite accurately the policy said the Soviet leadership had not weakened its commitment to Communist goals or political or ideological competition with the west.

For having the nerve to say that my colleague was roundly denounced by both Senator Evans[3] and the Prime Minister[4]. According to them he was living in the past and utterly out of touch.

Equal scorn has been heaped on Mr Spender, myself and others for actually questioning the wisdom of fishing agreements with the Soviet Union. Bill Hayden[5] even had qualms about

---

[3] Senator the Honourable Gareth Evans, AC, KC, Labor Senator for Victoria, Attorney-General of Australia, 2 September 1988 – 11 March 1996.

[4] The Honourable Bob Hawke AC, 23rd Prime Minister of Australia, 11 March 1983 – 20 December 1991.

[5] The Honourable Bill Hayden AC, Minister for Foreign Affairs and Trade, 11 March 1983 – 17 August 1988 later the 21st Governor-General of Australia.

these several years ago. He warned Pacific Island states about their dangers.

Mikhail Gorbachev[6] is a totally new phenomenon for a Soviet leader. He is smarter and more attuned to western thinking than any of those before him. He shrewdly detects a desire by many in the West to want to believe that the Soviet Union has permanently changed whatever the real facts.

Even while he was waiting in the wings, he knew a different tack with the west was needed. His well-publicised meeting with Margaret Thatcher[7] which produced from her the famous 'I can do business with this man' line, clearly showed this.

Gorbachev's policies of Perestroika and Glasnost have begun to change the Soviet Union. The INF Treaty has given the world greater hope. It is everyone's wish that these hopes can be consolidated.

No-one who dreams of permanent peace would have been left unmoved by the immense imagery and symbolism of the Gorbachev/Reagan summits.

The sight of wind-swept Mikhail Gorbachev, Ronald Reagan[8] and George Bush[9] standing beneath the Statue of Liberty in New York harbour was very powerful stuff.

Gorbachev's disarmament offensive is welcome. It is a step forward, but it should always be understood for what it really is. Nor should we forget the context in which it occurred.

The Soviet leader has taken the strategic political decision that

---

[6] Mikhail Gorbachev, General Secretary of the Communist Party of the Soviet Union, 11 March 1985 – 24 August 1991, President of the Soviet Union, 15 March 1990 – 25 December 1991.

[7] The Right Honourable The Baroness Thatcher, Prime Minister of the United Kingdom, 4 May 1979 – 28 November 1990.

[8] Ronald Reagan, 40th President of the United States, January 20, 1981 – January 20, 1989.

[9] George H.W. Bush, 43rd Vice President of the United States later 41st President of the United States, January 20, 1989 – January 20, 1993.

his country's economy cannot bear the burden of matching the military potential of the United States. Having reached this decision he has made a public relations virtue out of that economic necessity. All the evidence is that he has been stunningly successful.

Reading some of the rave reviews from a personality driven western media one is tempted to think that the Soviet leader has learnt more from Madison Avenue than he ever learnt from Marx.

Many western commentators are only too happy to depict the United States and the Soviet Union as having morally equivalent political systems. They have given Gorbachev virtually all of the credit for an historic turnaround in the arms race.

They have completely forgotten the Reagan/Weinberger[10] factor. The Reagan dual track approach worked. He strengthened the United States through the strategic modernisation programme. He shored-up NATO and argued rationally against the unilateral disarmers.

At the same time, he was willing to talk but from a position of strength. Many have forgotten that the Soviets walked out of disarmament talks in 1983 only to return several years later. United States determination under Reagan forced the Soviets back to the negotiating table.

It was that strength – not ideological conversion – which has induced Mikhail Gorbachev to bring about the apparently profound but nonetheless totally managed change of direction in the Soviet Union.

Enormous change has taken place under Gorbachev. The astonishing sight of open debate on Soviet television is something undreamt of only a few years ago. There is more freedom of speech than before.

---

[10] Caspar Weinberger, 15th United States Secretary of Defense, January 21, 1981 – November 23, 1987.

By the same token the mass experiments with private enterprise and capitalism which occurred in China only a few years ago left a lot of people in the west gasping for breath. They also made many reformers in the eastern bloc countries very envious.

Given the nature of totalitarian states the relative openness we now see in the Soviet Union is not one that will ever admit of a truly democratic revolution.

The evidence so far is that Gorbachev and the Soviet leadership have taken the strategic political decision that Peristroika and Glasnost are critical to the survival of Communist party hegemony. Their adoption does not represent an ideological conversion to liberal democracy.

To enter these reservations is not to argue against reaching agreements with the Soviet Union where those agreements are soundly based. We should seek a close relationship with the Soviet people.

We should never deal with other nations purely on the basis of ideology. That is absurd and self-defeating.

Likewise, we should never forget that profound ideological differences do exist between the liberal democracies of the west and totalitarian countries.

That so many heads are now being shaken in disbelief at what is occurring in China suggests that we may have gone too far down the path of removing ideology from our assessments of nations.

Perhaps having done it with China let us not repeat the mistake with the Soviet Union.

*****

Friday, 16 June 1989, p. 13

3

A welfare system more obsessed with rules than reality requires a new way of thinking, according to Howard. With first-hand experience of the work of local charities and voluntary welfare organisations in his electorate and throughout Australia, Howard ponders whether the welfare sector might even become the new frontier of the privatisation debate.

'The dry way to warmer welfare'

'It's time we looked at a bit of privatisation of the welfare sector'

Several months ago, I met representatives of non-government welfare bodies to discuss the Burdekin Report on homeless young people.

The frustration felt by many dedicated people in the welfare area with the existing system was summed up in one story told at that meeting.

Two young kids were literally taken off the streets by an officer of an organisation without peer in both experience and integrity in the welfare field anywhere in Australia.

'The rules' prevented the organisation giving those young people financial help, arranging a foster home for them, or providing them with ongoing shelter – however temporary.

Due to their age the agency had to report all the details to the Department of Youth and Community Services which promptly returned the young people to the foster homes from which they had fled. Within two days the same young people were back on the streets and the cycle commenced again.

I have no doubt there are good reasons why the department should be notified. The young people were minors. I am not having a cheap shot at the bureaucracy.

Nonetheless, the incident portrayed a system more obsessed with rules than reality.

That story set me thinking as to whether or not part of the problem with our welfare system at present is that we don't put enough trust and confidence in the judgement, experience, discretion, cost consciousness and compassion of our great and reputable voluntary welfare organisations.

Put another way, isn't it time we looked at indulging ourselves in a little bit of privatisation of the welfare sector.

The welfare sector might even become the new frontier of the privatisation debate.

Privatisation is well and truly on the political agenda.

There is still plenty of huffing and puffing left in that debate so far as it affects government commercial operations. However, it is no longer a question of whether, but when, privatisation of commercial operations occurs.

If the Hawke Government does not fully or partially privatise Qantas and Australian Airlines before the next election, then a new Coalition government will implement its detailed privatisation programme which has been on its policy books for two to three years.

That whole debate has come a long way since 1985. Then, not only the ALP ranted and raved about the evils of privatisation, but many Liberals were cowed into either silence or outright opposition by the campaign of fear and loathing then waged by the Labor Party and the unions.

Majority community opinion now accepts that it is absurd to inject huge volumes of budget dollars into airlines and banks when the latter could be out there in the market competing for those funds.

The ultimate justification for selling the Commonwealth Bank or Qantas is not the money received for selling those assets, however valuable that is in reducing our existing stock of debt.

The prime reason is to give the customer a better deal. If a privatisation proposal cannot meet this test then there is serious doubt as to whether it should go ahead.

If the management of Qantas and Australian Airlines are to be believed, then the customers of those two airlines will be much better off after privatisation.

Amongst other things the airlines will have the cash to buy more aircraft and provide more diverse services. Their maintenance will be better because they will have the flexibility to pay more competitive wages for skilled mechanics. Ongoing safety is very relevant to airline customers – particularly regular ones!

Whilst it is never quite put in those words, the same criterion of giving the customer or recipient a better deal applies to welfare services as well.

In suggesting that we consider further privatisation of welfare services I am not reaching for an axe to hack indiscriminately at welfare.

'Volunteer bodies deal with the person – not the file'

Moreover, what I have in mind would actually involve voluntary organisations having the authority to make on-the-spot decisions about the spending of taxpayers' money.

I am not suggesting that a greater financial burden be thrown on these bodies.

The past 20 years has seen a huge rise in the welfare bill, a rapid expansion of the welfare bureaucracy, with all the rivalries and duplication which that entails, and sadly the growth of a large under-class who have experienced nothing but welfare dependency.

The reasons for this are legion. What I canvass here is a modest proposal not pretending for a moment that it alone can reverse a 20-year trend.

At the core of the privatisation debate is always the basic question. Will privatisation be to the public benefit?

In the case of welfare – particularly that involving crisis support – the question is whether a greater role for the voluntary bodies will benefit the people needing help?

I suspect the answer is yes. It is at least worth a try.

Bodies such as the Salvation Army, the Sydney City Mission and St Vincent de Paul, by dint of their experience in the field, know more about real poverty, deprivation and personal tragedy than any others in our society. Equally, they are more skilled at spotting a bludger than most public servants.

There are some bureaucrats imbued with the philosophy that welfare is an automatic entitlement and not something which provides temporary support until the normal pattern of self support can be resumed. They have neither the skill nor the motivation to weed out the genuine from the imposter.

Voluntary bodies bring to the problem a wonderful blend of hard-headedness and compassion. They know the value of a dollar because it is theirs. They have had to raise it. Through years of experience, they have had to direct their limited financial resources to areas of maximum need.

They are on the job 365 days a year and know where the real priorities are. They are not burdened by massive bureaucratic structures when they are confronted with a person in crisis. They deal with the person and the crisis – not with the file.

This is not a total denunciation of all government welfare efforts. Nor am I suggesting that the payment of old age pensions be taken over from the Department of Social Security by the Smith Family.

There is no feasible alternative to the present administrative system of paying most income support benefits.

What I propose involves non-government organisations having the power, in certain cases, to decide that cash support from taxpayers' funds should be given to individuals – that they have the authority to determine entitlements at least on a temporary basis.

Shock – horror – radicalism to some no doubt, but not really.

To those who wail about public accountability I simply reply – VEDC[11] and Western Australian Inc! After these two inglorious examples of politicians and public servants sending millions of dollars of taxpayers' money down the drain, let any bureaucrat or politician dare to question the capacity of the Salvation Army or the St Vincent de Paul to make sensible decisions about the payment of modest amounts of taxpayers' money.

With this general approach in mind, let us return to the story at the beginning.

The voluntary organisation in question should have been able to provide temporary shelter. It should have been able to decide whether some crisis financial support be given and generally held the two young people within its care until some investigations were carried out.

It would not be asking too much to trust the judgement and discretion of our greatest welfare agencies. It would not be a misuse of taxpayers' money to allow them to make certain decisions on the spot. Of course, they would need to account, and of course they would need to be hard-headed.

We can also be certain that allowing such organisations a bigger say in the crisis welfare field will ensure that the highest possible premium is put on reuniting families where this is possible.

Welfare targeting is an endless debate. Any rigid set of entitlement rules will cover the great bulk of cases.

However, things are different in crisis welfare situations.

---

[11] Victorian Economic Development Corporation (VEDC)

The remoteness of the decision maker from the potential recipient will increase the likelihood of error. It will magnify the possibility of injustices in one case and waste in another.

An efficient, targeted and just welfare system will more likely exist if we supplement general eligibility rules with much greater flexibility in crisis welfare situations.

This must mean giving our voluntary welfare bodies more power and more discretion. It is their greater coal face experience which best enables them to make skilful, compassionate judgements in individual cases.

Why don't we entrust to those who have a moral commitment to helping others, greater authority to make decisions about who gets welfare support?

My hunch is that this process will also save some money.

More importantly, it will do more to help people help themselves. Ultimately that ought to be the goal of any compassionate and efficient welfare system.

*****

Friday, 23 June 1989, p. 13

4

Recognising all politics is local, Howard nominates 'trade, trees, and trains' as issues to dominate national politics in the 1990s. With economic chaos flourishing, greenhouse effect a rising trend, and increasing crime due to drugs, Howard calls for action on high interest rates, balanced and sensitive environmental policies, and an integrated national approach to law enforcement.

'Integrate - or disintegrate'

Over a drink at this week's Liberal federal council, a company director asked me what issues I thought would dominate national politics over the next ten years.

Rather facetiously I said trade, trees and trains. On reflection, I am not sure that observation was so flippant.

This week's record current account deficit again demonstrated that we have a gigantic trade problem which lies at the root of the economic chaos now enveloping Australia, paralysing the Hawke Government, and putting home ownership beyond the reach of ordinary Australians.

While we buy more than we sell and need to borrow the savings of foreigners to make up the difference, we will be plagued by high interest rates.

No practising politician needs an opinion poll to show how dominant the environment has now become as a political issue.

Some of the most shellback conservatives I know have taken to sprouting forth about the need for balanced and sensitive environmental policies.

They are right. I share their concern. Immediately after the

1987 election I encouraged the Liberal Party to develop a more sympathetic policy in this area which has now been done.

Indeed, the Liberal Party, at my behest, led the way in articulating opposition to mining in the Antarctic.

A real concern, I have, however, is that the issue will become so trendy that any proposition with the label 'environment' will win superficial acceptance.

'Petty jealousies are unacceptable'.

The widely publicised TV presentation 'Climate in Crisis' which drew enormous ratings was a case in point. School children were duly encouraged to view it.

I watched and found it a big disappointment. It was all rhetoric and pretty footage. The programme was based on the arrogant presumption that all its viewers tamely accepted that there was a greenhouse effect.

No technical evidence establishing the greenhouse effect was put forward. It was all based on assertion.

There is persuasive evidence that the greenhouse effect is not just a slogan.

However, like all propositions of its kind it must be sustained by proper intellectual argument otherwise over time it will be rejected.

When I moved on to trains my business colleague at the Federal Council thought that like Mussolini[12], I wanted the trains to run on time. I said that making travel on trains safer from hooligans and thugs was what I had in mind.

Fear for the safety of body and property is dominant for a growing number of Australians in our major cities. The poorer one is, the greater the vulnerability.

They are scared in the suburbs. They are scared to travel in

[12] Benito Mussolini, Prime Minister of Italy, 31 October 1922 – 25 July 1943.

trains late at night. They worry about the safety of their children. The midday household robbery has become commonplace.

No longer can one sleep with the door open on a hot night.

Australians resent the loss of this innocence. They know the clock cannot be turned back but they would massively support a political party which asserted the most fundamental of all responsibilities, that is the physical security of its citizens.

George Bush ran hard and effectively on law and order. Nick Greiner's[13] sweep of the western suburbs last year owed much to the rising tide of resentment about crime.

One of the ironies of government over the past twenty years has been that simultaneously with the rise in both the size and complexity of the bureaucracy there has been a sharp fall in the apparent effectiveness of basic law enforcement.

This is perplexing bearing in mind that protecting people and their property is the most basic of all responsibilities of government.

Nothing better illustrates the futility of much of modern government than the squandering of scarce resources on social engineering while core obligations such as law enforcement appear to languish.

Some of the malaise flows from relatively poor pay for police. Some of it is due to the law enforcement agencies being hobbled by Marquis of Queensberry rules while criminals have had open slather.

Much of it has been due to the social disintegration through the erosion of family authority and the insidious rise in drug abuse.

Moreover, in Australia I don't believe our federal system has helped.

State/Federal jealousies are probably inevitable on many issues but, when it comes to fighting crime, they ought to be unacceptable.

---

[13] The Honourable Nick Greiner AC, Premier of New South Wales, 25 March 1988 – 24 June 1992.

The wrangling over the National Crime Authority which saw State governments of both political persuasions fighting to preserve their respective cow patches was a good illustration of the problem.

The rivalries between State and Federal police have become legendary in a number of areas.

For a nation of 16 million people whose drug traffickers know nothing of such colonial niceties as state boundaries, any fragmentation of the law enforcement effort can only be good news for criminals.

This is not a call for a complete federal takeover. It is, however, a plea for an integrated national approach.

A truly national approach can be achieved without Canberra grabbing all the power.

Despite some weaknesses the co-operative Companies and Securities scheme has worked well. It is a vast improvement on the disjointed, uncoordinated system which preceded it.

We should take a more integrated national approach to law enforcement.

This applies particularly to fighting the drug traffic. It is undeniably a national problem. Heroin is an imported substance, and the Federal Government has a compelling responsibility.

There is even a division of responsibilities with duplicated effort and a waste of administrative resources within some State governments.

There ought to be a single, national, cohesive body to tackle the problem, not the myriad of agencies at a State and Federal level which is currently the situation.

It should be a joint Commonwealth/State body. It should have a national commitment to the extermination of the biggest single threat which exists to our social stability.

The petty jealousies which pervade Canberra, Spring Street

and Macquarie Street – whomever is in power – might be tolerable on some issues. When it comes literally to the murder of our youth no Australian should tolerate them any longer.

It will be greatly to the moral credit of the political party which takes a strong stand on this issue.

It will also be good politics.

Trains will be very much on the political agenda in the 1990's.

*****

Friday, 30 June 1989, p. 11

5

Monopoly trade union power on the rise while membership levels are decreasing has Howard asking who is running the country.

'Something wrong with the state of the union'

The most important figure for the Australian economy released by the Australian Statistician recently was not the record current account deficit for May, horrendous though it was. Rather it was his data on trade union membership published several weeks ago.

That data showed only 42 per cent of the workforce belonged to trade unions down from a figure of 51 per cent in 1976.

Significantly the percentage of the private sector workforce belonging to unions had fallen to only 32. In 1982 it was 39 per cent.

Most revealing of all was the massive rejection of trade unionism by the young. Only 32 per cent of those under 25 held union tickets, down from 43 per cent in 1976.

When proper allowance is made for *de facto* compulsory unionism via the closed shop or otherwise, which exists in many industries, these are very dismal figures for the union enthusiast.

They tell us a lot about the intrinsic hostility of average Australians to trade union bosses.

What makes the figures remarkable is that this big decline in the number of Australians belonging to unions has occurred at the very same time as the institutional power of trade unions in our country has flourished and increased.

In other words, as unions have become less popular, they have been given more power by the government.

As everyone knows, the Australian Council of Trade Unions (ACTU) has become part of the Hawke Government. The unelected Simon Crean[14] and Bill Kelty[15] wield more influence than the Labor Caucus and all but a handful of senior ministers.

Yet this is the case when fewer and fewer Australians want to belong to trade unions.

This has not only produced perverse economic consequences it is also democratically perverse.

The notion that any section of the community, however numerically strong or popular, should enjoy a legal privilege over the rest of the community ought to be abhorrent.

Yet the trade union movement has always had an elite legal status in the Australian community. On occasions this has been tempered by such measures as Section 45D of the Trade Practices Act. There is no doubt that the Hawke Government has entrenched the privileged position of the union movement since coming to power.

When it is now realised that since 1983 Australians have voted with their feet against unions, that situation becomes – to use a term beloved of the Prime Minister – quite obscene.

This amazing paradox whereby the trade union movement's authority, power and influence has varied in inverse proportion to its public acceptability is rooted in the strongly authoritarian view of the role of the trade union movement adhered to by the political and industrial wings of the labour movement.

As Minister for Business and Consumer Affairs[16] I encountered that view in 1977 when introducing Section 45D to the Trade Practices Act which prohibited secondary boycotts by trade unions.

---

[14] The Honourable Simon Crean, President of the ACTU, 1 March 1985 – 25 March 1990 later a minister in the Hawke, Keating, Rudd, and Gillard governments: Leader of the Opposition, 22 November 2001 – 2 December 2003.

[15] Secretary of the ACTU from 1983 to 2000.

[16] 22 December 1975 – 17 July 1977.

The peak union movement councils were consulted about the legislation, and I still vividly recall the violent reaction of the then ACTU president, Mr Hawke, and his public service counterpart.

What I shall always remember is the sheer incredulity they expressed at the very thought of any activity of a trade union being subjected in any way to the processes of the ordinary courts of Australia.

That view has persisted. It found expression in the 1985 Hancock Committee Report, which formed the basis of the Hawke Government's Industrial Relations Act passed last year substantially rewriting our industrial relations laws.

The Hancock Committee report contained the astounding proposition that trade unions should not be subjected to the ordinary courts of Australia because they were strong enough to defy the judgements of those courts.

It is worth quoting the committee's explanation of this quite breathtaking proposition.

> 'If we ask why litigants and sportsmen usually accept the adjudicators' decisions, we find part of the answer in the ethics accepted by the disputants; but part, too, lies in their relative weakness.

'Numbers are declining but power grows and flourishes'

> The two factors are interrelated: the ethic of accepting decisions gains strength from the difficulty of doing otherwise. By contrast, trade unions are, to varying degrees, centres of power: they replace the powerlessness of individual workers with collective strength. It is a mistaken view of the pluralistic society to assume that every 'subject' is equally dominated by the might of the State and its arms of enforcement. Some may wish that things were different: but vain hopes are no basis for effective policy.'

Such a rationale ought to be totally rejected by any truly liberal democracy.

However, even if we accept its logic for the moment, that logic itself must now be seriously in question given the steady decline in the number of people who belong to trade unions.

At what point, a la Hancock, does the trade union movement become weak enough to be brought within the reach of the ordinary courts of Australia?

All of this begs a basic question, that is, the power of the trade union movement in our community and the need to reduce that power as an integral element of deregulating our industrial relations system.

The dreadful trade figures which batter the national psychic of Australia every month are a symptom of a deep economic illness.

That illness will not be cured by flashy fine tuning, nor will the virus be extinguished by killing the patient with continued high interest rates.

The illness is one of low productivity. We continue to consume more than we produce – not because our appetite for consumption is grotesque or avaricious by western standards.

Rather it is because we do not produce enough and until we remove those impediments to higher productivity, we will continue to experience a fall in living standards.

Moreover, we will resort to the short term expedient of killing off import demand to temporarily relieve our balance of payments, only to start the cycle all over again.

Our economic problem is a structural and not a cyclical one.

Three years ago, Mr Hawke told us it was all because the foreigners paid us too little for our commodities. Almost immediately they started paying us decent prices, yet the problem did not go away.

Some very painful and difficult adjustment is needed. It is needed more urgently now than it was several years ago because some precious years have been lost.

However much some may wish to run away from it and however

beckoning the comfortable life of the industrial relations consensus may be, the reality is that deregulating our labour market remains the single most important economic challenge Australia faces.

Let's not delude ourselves. Deregulating that market involves reducing the institutional power of trade unions in Australia.

Until we confront and solve this problem, we won't achieve a more productive Australian economy.

Freeing-up our labour market will sweep away many of the restrictive practices which continue to retard productivity growth.

Those who think otherwise should have a look at our productivity performance over the past few years. They should have a look at what the Accord has done to Australian productivity.

They should have a look at the giant productivity strides made by British manufacturing industry in the more deregulated industrial relations environment of the Thatcher years.

This is not a call to arms against trade unionists or trade unionism.

Individual workers have much to gain from a deregulated labour market.

Profit sharing and employee-ownership carry enormous incentives for workers.

Freeing the labour market will not reduce the living standards of employees. Over time, through higher productivity, it will enhance them.

It will undeniably challenge the citadels of power of the trade union elite. This is only to be expected. They have privileges and influence denied to others.

This ought to be all the more offensive now that the troops themselves are throwing away their arms and deserting their trade union generals.

They are losing faith in the cause.

*****

JULY 1989

Friday, 7 July 1989, p. 15

6

Environment issues are now mainstream … be careful what you wish for, cautions Howard.

'It's our business to unite on laws'

Green is beautiful. That is the clear political message driven home in such spectacular fashion by the watershed Tasmanian election. No politician in any Australian political party should think otherwise.

The new mark of a macho politician in Australia is whether or not he has brought forth the toughest environmental regulations on a particular subject not just in Australia but anywhere in the world.

So rapidly has the environment scooted to the top of the political pops that governments (and oppositions) are literally falling over themselves to show the strength of their commitment to the environment.

Much of this is good and should be welcomed.

No longer is concern for the environment seen as a trendy issue on the periphery of politics. It has gone mainstream. That was only too evident during the Tasmanian election campaign and in the result of that election itself.

But going mainstream carries certain responsibilities.

One of those responsibilities is to match the rhetoric with solid arguments. As I observed in an earlier column, there wasn't much evidence of this in the widely viewed TV programme 'Climate in Crisis'.

There is little point in mouthing platitudes about the greenhouse effect without some solid facts.

Another critical responsibility is to know the cost of environmental protection and see it is fairly shared.

Most importantly also the cost should be no greater than necessary.

Unless we are very careful Australia will end up with a hotch-potch of environmental laws as the six State governments and the Federal government compete with each other to see who can provide the most stringent environmental requirements.

This may gladden the hearts of some who would be happy to stop much development dead in its tracks. The majority, however, would come to think otherwise.

The result would be massive additional and unnecessary costs imposed on business and through charges to the consumer ultimately upon the general public. There would also be a huge cost through lost investment and employment opportunities.

Community concern about the environment is powerful enough to make reasonable extra costs publicly acceptable. The research carried out by the Greiner government regarding sewerage pollution seemed to suggest this.

However, a special levy on water rates to pay for a beach clean-up is overt and clear.

The hidden costs of a labyrinth of overlapping State and Federal environmental rules is another thing altogether.

Unfortunately, most State governments will believe there is political mileage in going it alone with their own environmental protection laws. The environment-conscious public may as a result think you are purer on the subject than any of the others.

'It is ludicrous to set company different guidelines for States and Commonwealth.'

This political disincentive against uniformity of laws throughout Australia could become a new regulatory nightmare for many Australian companies.

We had a little taste this week.

Tim Moore, the New South Wales Environment Minister, wants all of the other States to adopt his anti-pollution laws. He says they are the toughest in the world – a familiar refrain these days on any environmental matter.

He's having trouble with Western Australia. The government of that State claims to have been ahead of the game by bringing in tough anti-pollution laws three years ago.

Now I have no idea who deserves to be in the Guinness Book of Records on this one.

What I do know is that kind of Dutch auction is a potent brew for ugly and costly lack of uniformity of laws concerning the environment throughout Australia.

There are enough extra costs imposed on business already by such things as our highly regulated industrial relations system, an over-regulated transport sector and many far from uniform corporate regulations.

These are some of the imposts which make Australian industries uncompetitive and help create our trade problems. We would be crazy to add to these burdens the extra cost of requiring companies doing business in Australia to comply with different environmental laws in different States.

This is not a plea against effective environmental laws and requirements. That we should have a proper balance between environmental protection and economic development is beyond argument.

Rather, it is a plea that in the process of trying to outdo each other in scoring political points on the environment, the governments of Australia don't lead us to a new chaos of conflicting and disuniform laws.

The experience to date is depressing.

Wesley Vale was hopelessly botched because there was no political will on the part of either the former Tasmanian government or the Hawke government to work together. They tried to wrong-foot each other and ended up losing a pulp mill they both said they wanted.

There should have been a common environmental code between them.

It is ludicrous to ask a company to satisfy one set of environmental guidelines for a State government and then to go through the same process in relation to a different set of guidelines with the Federal government.

That is what occurred in relation to Wesley Vale. It was obvious it was going to happen yet each of the two governments allowed it to occur.

Likewise is the situation for a company operating nationally and having to comply with differing environmental laws from State to State.

The extra costs could be crippling.

The headlines tell us that the Prime Minister wants a lead role on the world environment scene. That's a worthy goal.

Perhaps for the moment he should set his sights a little more modestly. He should aim for a lead role on the Australian environmental scene by seeing to it that we have uniform, orderly and cost-efficient environmental regulations throughout Australia.

It won't be easy. It's hard enough securing agreement between the Federal government and the States when there is no political incentive to be different.

Just recall the tortuous path to uniform company law. We still don't have uniform defamation laws. National credit laws took ages.

The reality, however, is that unless we have effective uniformity in the environmental area then the cost burdens could become unacceptably high.

The buck does stop with the Federal government. There is now strong bipartisan acceptance that concern for the environment is a national issue.

I do not believe in future a rabid States rights argument about the environment will make anything like the impact it did some years ago.

There is a healthy new consensus on this issue.

The government could still blow this consensus by trying to deal with the problem by holding a referendum with the next Federal election. That would be an overkill and would be rightly seen as a Canberra power grab. It would certainly be defeated, and that defeat would undermine prospects for bipartisan and Federal/State co-operation.

This problem calls for effective leadership and co-operative effort – not political posturing.

Mr Hawke has promised us the greatest ever environmental statement delivered by any government anywhere in the world.

Surely something as impressive as that has room within it for a statement as to how the Federal government will achieve and maintain uniform environmental laws within Australia.

*****

Friday, 14 July 1989, p. 11

7

As re-regulatory rumbles grow louder, financial re-regulation is not the answer to Australia's economic mayhem, argues Howard. The answer is further deregulation of our 'rigid' labour market. There is no turning back.

'Why a return to the cocktail hour will give us a hangover'

We don't hear the expression 'cocktail' anymore when talk turns to housing interest rates.

We used to in the early 1980's. It described a loan package from a bank where some of the loan was at the artificially low regulated rate and the rest of the loan from the bank's finance company affiliate was at a much higher rate.

The average cost of the loan turned out to be the then market rate.

It would be a good idea if those people in all political parties who think the answer to high interest rates is a dose of financial re-regulation were to study the causes of cocktail loans some years ago.

Then, as now, interest rates were high. At that time, unlike the present, banks were heavily regulated being subject to both interest rate and quantitative lending controls.

If you wanted a housing loan the banks could not help you much because they had very little money to lend.

Due to interest rate ceilings, the banks couldn't offer market rates to get adequate deposits. Most of the deposits went to the non-bank financial institutions which were unregulated.

Many of those institutions did not lend for housing.

If you wanted a housing loan from your bank you had to take a cocktail loan.

In other words, heavy regulation through interest rate ceilings did not protect new borrowers against high interest rates. It merely rationed deposits away from banks.

The big difference now is that the banks have got most of the deposits. Due to deregulation, they can offer market rates for funds.

So bringing back controls won't shield us from high interest rates.

Such controls might affect the patterns of lending within the community but they won't alter the end price of money. That is a function of general economic conditions.

The re-regulatory rumbles are growing louder.

Debate on this issue goes to the heart of what happens to the Australian economy over the next ten years.

As we gaze with increasingly boggled eyes at a mounting foreign debt there will be no shortage of economic quacks.

If the wrong turn is taken by Australia on the issue of economic regulation, then we will be in even bigger trouble than we are now.

Basically, there are three options.

First, we can rest on the oars of the present level of deregulation and Micawber-like hope that something will turn up.

That's what the Hawke government has elected to do. The evidence so far is that this is not a very impressive option.

'The only feasible option is to push on and complete the deregulation of our economy'

Second, we can wind back the clock by re-regulating in the mistaken belief that the problems we now have are a product of deregulation. That's the cocktail option.

The third option is to finish the deregulatory job by freeing up those areas of the economy which remain in the collectivist grip. In particular, we can do something really decisive about our rigid labour markets.

The most depressing element of this whole debate is the abysmal ignorance of so many as to what causes Australia's overseas debt.

That debt is not caused by entrepreneurs borrowing overseas.

We have a huge overseas debt because the payments we make for imports, services and debt charges exceed our export receipts.

The difference must be financed in some way. In borrowing overseas Messrs Murdoch, Brierly, Packer, et al are merely part of the financing process.

I was left breathless this week by a report of Stewart West's[17] economic paper which argues that controls on foreign borrowings are justified because of the contribution of private foreign debt to Australia's current account deficit.

It is incredible that a cabinet minister in a government which has been in office through the worst current account crisis since the 1930's should be so ignorant about the fundamentals of that crisis.

Australia can restrict private overseas borrowings if it wishes.

There would be a number of interesting results, including some increased pressure on domestic interest rates and the exchange rate. But one can be absolutely certain that one of the results would not be any sustainable improvement in our current account deficit.

The current account problem Australia now faces results from low productivity. It is caused by an excess of demand over output.

The defeatist solution is to give up on productivity and permanently opt for a lower standard of living by depressing consumption.

---

[17] Member for Cunningham (NSW), 15 October 1977 – 8 February 1993 and minister in the Hawke Government.

In the short term that is what the Hawke government is now doing. It is using high interest rates to squeeze enough life out of the economy to reduce demand and bring the current account deficit within manageable proportions.

It's a very dicey approach. Not only can it fall foul of overkill, but it is not part of a longer term programme to make the economy productive.

If the community saw high interest rates as an unavoidable short-term element of an economic vision to put Australia on a sounder productive base, then I believe there would be more public acceptance of the present level of interest rates.

This is not the case. There is no economic encore after high interest rates have done their job.

Do we start the process all over again? Do we allow demand once more to gather pace only to be squashed again because it is surging ahead of output?

Only next time in the absence of policy changes the cycle will be shorter. Our debt levels will see to that.

The Hawke government rightly deserves credit for dumping its earlier opposition to financial deregulation and embracing the Campbell Committee reforms.

The Treasurer[18] and the ACTU Secretary, Mr Kelty, are absolutely right when they say that the Australian economy has been internationalised and that there is no turning back.

Mr Keating is also right to reject the flimsy economic gimmickry being urged upon him by his party colleagues.

However, the Treasurer is completely wrong in believing that the process of deregulation has gone far enough, that the necessary structural adjustments have been made and that all he must do is hang on and in a few months' time all will be well.

---

[18] The Honourable Paul Keating, Treasurer of Australia, 11 March 1983 – 3 June 1991 and 24th Prime Minister of Australia, 20 December 1991 – 11 March 1996.

The only bacon which will come home to the Treasurer in the next few months will be very rancid.

We must surely accept that the real economic challenge is to create a more productive Australian economy which enables us to earn enough in the future to pay for a high level of consumption – that is to have a high living standard. That being the case, the only feasible option for Australia is to push ahead and complete the deregulation of our economy.

Financial deregulation exposed us, warts and all, to the rest of the world.

It's not that we weren't part of the world before financial deregulation, but pre 1983 the signals were less direct, and we did not always feel the need to adjust quite so rapidly to changes elsewhere.

The external freeing of the Australian economy cried aloud for matching internal deregulation.

The warts it exposed included a rigid industrial relations system built on excessive trade union power.

They included a system where it costs more to carry cargo from Burnie in Tasmania to Newcastle than it does to carry cargo from Newcastle to Los Angeles. They included a tax system which scares off savers.

Forging an economy which rewards greater output through an enterprise-based industrial relations system will take time and will be resisted by power groups in the community.

There must be an absolute recognition that in the medium term no improvement in living standards can be achieved and that perhaps they will fall further before we turn the corner.

That might sound unduly gloomy, but it is unavoidable. The cocktail option won't work, and it is self-evident that just as you can't be half pregnant, you can't half deregulate the economy.

Pressure on either side of politics to reduce the momentum for economic change must be resisted.

That is why growing support for some re-regulation of the financial system is so insidious.

It is the politics of believing that in the modern world a return to the old, cossetted days is the answer to our predicament.

*****

Friday, 21 July 1989, p. 17

8

With media shining a light on political corruption in Japan and Queensland, Howard defends the right of people to no longer tolerate unethical conduct by elected officials and to demand official action. But is a federal-ICAC the answer?

'Sun rising on a new era'

Just imagine Senator Button[19] saying 'I think the ALP should give up power to the Opposition. We of the ALP want to get out of office and reconstruct ourselves'.

If anyone thinks the Prime Minister was a bit rough on John Button for having the honesty to admit that the ALP's re-election chances were no better than 50/50, you can imagine the wrath which would descend on the Senate leader if he uttered those words.

He hasn't, of course. To be fair to the Senator it's not likely that he ever will.

However, with the substitution of LDP for ALP those words were uttered a bare two weeks ago by a senior member of the Japanese government, the Minister for Trade and Industry, Mr Kajiyama.[20]

He was, of course, speaking of the enormous political difficulties now faced by the ruling Liberal Democratic Party government in Japan.

That party which has governed Japan since 1948 has been reeling for months from the so-called Recruit scandal.

---

[19] The Honourable John Button, Labor Senator for Victoria, 18 May 1974 – 31 March 1993 and minister in the Hawke and Keating governments.

[20] Seiroku Kajiyama, a member of Takeshita and Uno cabinets, 1987-1990.

The sheer desperation of Mr Kajiyama's comments shows how deeply this scandal has bitten into the psyche of the LDP.

The government faces an Upper House election on 23 July which all commentators suggest will involve a severe drubbing and a loss of LDP control of that House.

Most indications are that the Japanese Prime Minister, Mr Uno[21], who has only been in power a matter of weeks, will be forced to resign after the expected Upper House debacle.

His apparently imminent demise coming hard on the heels of Mr Takeshita's[22] fall from grace will mean that a new era in Japanese politics will have really arrived.

By that I don't mean the likely election of a Socialist or other non-Liberal Democratic Party government. If that does happen, it will be yet another new era so to speak.

That the Takeshita/Uno debacle should have occurred, and the manner of its occurring, show that much has changed in Japanese politics.

In particular, it shows a dramatic change in ethical standards under the influence of vigorous scrutiny by the media.

On the other hand, some features of the saga demonstrate very clearly that certain things haven't and won't change.

Takeshita was forced out because he was compelled to admit having taken money from the Recruit organisation.

He and his associates received money which had been given to buy political and government favours.

According to any orthodox measurement of human conduct, it was corrupt and he deserved at the very least to go in disgrace from public life. So did his associates caught in the same act.

His chief of staff committed suicide. That kind of devotion is unheard of in Australian politics!

---

[21] Sosuke Uno, Prime Minister of Japan, 3 June 1989 – 10 August 1989.

[22] Noboru Takeshita, Prime Minister of Japan, 6 November 1987 – 3 June 1989.

The extraordinary aspect about the Recruit scandal was that there was nothing novel in Japan about the overt buying of political favours and support.

Past battles within the LDP for the top party post and hence the Japanese prime ministership have been characterised by huge sums of money passing hands to secure votes in leadership contests.

It has been open, well documented and a constant feature of Japanese politics for a long time.

Likewise has been the role within the LDP of the powerful beef lobby. Its financial clout has sealed the export fate of many an Australian cattleman over the years.

Therefore, the Recruit scandal was different only in degree – certainly not kind – from what has been accepted practice for decades in Japan.

That the Japanese public should have finally become impatient with those practices is both remarkable and healthy.

Just as the ABC Four Corners programme 'The Moonlight State' spilt the beans with a devastating effect on corruption in Queensland, the Japanese media played a crucial role in revving up public hostility over the recruit scandal.

The Four Corners programme was free and fearless journalism at its very best. It was an eloquent testimony as to what distinguishes a liberal democracy from authoritarian and totalitarian forms of government.

'Japanese politics will profit from this experience'

The parallels with Japan should not be pushed too far. However, in both cases the media provided a catalyst stirring and prodding so that official action became inevitable.

Politics in Japan will never be the same again.

The LDP will almost certainly go from office whenever a national poll is held.

Its inherited system of patronage and vote-buying will scarcely survive a period in opposition.

If Mr Kajiyama is right, the LDP will start to reconstruct itself. Japanese politics will profit from the experience, especially if the expected reconstruction opens the way for a new breed of LDP politician.

To start with, there may be a decisive break with the current habit whereby large numbers of senior Japanese politicians come direct from a bureaucracy where their behaviour is relatively free from scrutiny.

It is, of course, true that public hostility to the new 3 per cent turnover tax is one of the reasons the LDP has lost support.

However, the overwhelming cause of voter disillusionment surrounds the issue of ethics in government.

Just as the Fitzgerald inquiry in Queensland has forced the Queensland public to come to terms with what has been going on for years, so it is that publicity surrounding the Recruit scandal has driven home aspects of political life in Japan which hitherto the public has found too convenient to largely ignore.

So much for those things which have changed about Japanese political life.

The other side of the coin has been the way in which the whole episode has demonstrated the continuity with which things are done in Japan.

Despite months of scandal within the governing party, despite the forced resignation of a Prime Minister of less than 12 months and the likely oblivion of his successor, domestic and international confidence in the Japanese economy, and presumably the quality of its economic management, has hardly missed a beat.

Given the exceptional cosiness of the government/industry relationship in Japan one might have expected otherwise. The cynics will say that only proves again how irrelevant elected politicians have become in modern democracies.

That is cynical. It is not, however, entirely wrong so far as Japan is concerned.

All bureaucracies in industrial democracies are powerful. In Japan their authority is exceptional.

It is reinforced by the practice noted earlier of senior bureaucrats going direct into politics.

That the Japanese economy has remained so tranquil and undisturbed by recent events must testify both to its extraordinary strength as well as the dominant role of the Japanese bureaucracy.

The election of a Socialist government, indeed any non-LDP government, would be a phenomenon for democratic Japan. Such a possibility raises endless questions.

The Socialist Party has pledged to abolish the turnover tax. That might appear smart politics but is economically inept.

The historically high level of Japanese savings is being eroded by the ageing of the population.

A consumption tax is one way of slowing this trend.

Perhaps like other socialist governments it would change once in power.

By far the most likely change is that the continuity of personnel between the bureaucracy and politics will be sharply diminished if the LDP loses government.

Although the final impact of the Recruit scandal may take several years to be felt, already we can be certain that it has permanently changed public perceptions in Japan about what are acceptable standards and ethics in politics.

*****

Friday, 28 July 1989, p. 11

9

Embracing a view different to others is the cornerstone of Australian democracy, but not when it runs counter to the policies of the Hawke Government, argues Howard. Having delivered the first of his 'One Australia' speeches the previous year, Howard's ruminations about the deficiencies of multiculturalism were beginning to be exploited by his political opponents.

'Diversity yes; division never'

There are times when I think the late Senator Joseph McCarthy[23] should have been born in Australia. He would have done a roaring trade. One of the least attractive features of debate on public issues in Australia is the widespread use of the smear.

It happens with monotonous regularity on issues which have any degree of social sensitivity.

It is virtually impossible, for example, for anyone to question the existing priorities of the AIDS programme in Australia without being accused of a savage bias against homosexuals.

However, the prime area is surely that of multiculturalism – very much in the news this week. It is really quite impossible to question the philosophy of multiculturalism or indeed any aspect of multiculturalism without being accused of prejudice or intolerance towards Australians of non-Anglo-Celtic background.

That was my experience last year when I advocated a 'One Australia' philosophy which was subsequently entrenched in the opposition's immigration and ethnic affairs policy.

---

[23] United States Senator (Wisconsin), 3 January 1947 – 2 May 1957, and chair, Senate Government Operations Committee, 3 January 1953 – 3 January 1955.

A very plain-speaking Australian sporting hero, Rocky Gatellari[24], said it very bluntly last week.

Now, self-evidently, Rocky's ancestors didn't come from Yorkshire or Tipperary.

He gave some of the professional ethnics heaps and was very critical of self-appointed leaders of the ethnic community.

He made the significant point that it was difficult for those born in Australia to criticise aspects of the ethnic community without being labelled racist.

However much the apologists for the present policy of multiculturalism like to put it, they have surrounded their citadel with a barricade called anti-racism. If any critical voice is raised it is silenced by the pointed finger of 'you're a racist'.

The Prime Minister was at it again this week. Unless the opposition totally agreed with everything he said on multiculturalism it was being divisive.

The reservations I have about multiculturalism are not based on any desire to return Australia to the cultural mores of the 1940's. When I speak of One Australia, I do not have in mind a fixed Australian identity frozen on the dominant Anglo-Celtic 1940's.

Immigration from both Europe and Asia has enormously enriched, changed and strengthened Australia. That process will go on.

'One Australia is an inadequately explained ideal'

Some items in the Hawke multiculturalism agenda deserve support: a knowledge of English is an indispensable passport to fair treatment in Australia: full, fair and quick recognition of skills and qualifications gained overseas is part and parcel of workplace equality.

[24] Italian-Australian boxer, Olympian, political candidate, and businessman.

But a Multicultural Act? Will we have Multicultural Commission to administer that Act?

What is meant by 'reviews of the law and legal process and full administrative decision making from a multicultural point of view'.

That is surely vote-buying mumbo jumbo.

The One Australia philosophy I advocated last year was not a policy for Anglo-Celtic Australians. It was not anti-migrant. It included the emphatic declaration that all Australians were equal and entitled to a non-discriminatory life irrespective of their ethnic or religious background or place of birth.

More importantly, it was based upon the unshakeable belief I have that irrespective of one's ethnic background, all of us as Australians must be bound together by a set of common Australian values which take precedence over all other values and loyalties.

The first requirement of national self-confidence is a powerful conviction that the institutions, traditions and values of one's nation which make it distinctive are worth both preserving and exalting.

It is, after all, those very institutions, traditions and values which in the case of Australia have made her an attractive haven for millions from all corners of the world.

That other great immigrant story, the United States, has no trouble at all with these notions.

There is no more multicultural multiracial or cosmopolitan country in the world than the United States.

Yet unambiguously American nationalism and fierce commitment to distinctive American values and traditions claim the prime allegiance and loyalty of all its citizens irrespective of their ethnic background.

This occurs within an ambience of tolerance and non-discrimination.

Try as we may it is simply not possible to say that multiculturalism has yet delivered that result in Australia.

To say this is to run the risk of being called divisive.

Yet it is an argument which goes to national identity and national self-respect.

To me it is demeaning to tell the world that our national identity is nothing more than the sum total of fragments of one hundred and fifty other national identities.

Yet that is what multiculturalism seems to proclaim.

The perception many have of multiculturalism is that it extols ethnic diversity as the most important element of our national existence.

Our ethnic diversity should be extolled. It has made us a better country.

However, it is not and never can be our national cement any more than ethnic diversity is the national cement of the United States.

It is not something which makes us distinctively Australian. It is an aspect of our being Australian but only one aspect.

Racial tolerance is critical to a fair and just Australian society. So is tolerance of all kinds.

Political, religious and economic discrimination can be just as cruel and harmful as racial discrimination.

My quarrel with multiculturalism has not been its emphasis on diversity and tolerance.

It has been its elevation of diversity as the very essence of our Australian identity.

My concern is that in the process we have emphasised those things that divide and differentiate us as Australians rather than those things which unite us.

One Australia is an ideal. Like all ideals it is inadequately explained and widely misunderstood.

It is the ideal of a united nation composed of people of diverse ethnic backgrounds but bound together by an overriding commitment to institutions, traditions and values that are uniquely Australian and which claim their loyalties above all other loyalties.

One Australia speaks not of a fixed Australian identity but one constantly evolving and changing in response to many influences including a constant stream of immigration. However, that identity has as its essence values of fairness, mateship, enterprise, where necessary irreverence, and those other qualities which we know ourselves to be Australian and which mark us out around the world.

Ironically, at a time when Australian art and literature enjoys fashionable acceptance around the world precisely because of its distinctive Australian character, we seem to be allowing that distinctiveness to be blurred.

Moving from philosophical reservations multiculturalism has undoubtedly spawned a vast array of special interest groups.

By its character multiculturalism has built a new and powerful sectional interest.

New wants, new budget demands and new ambit claims are being made.

Government will be set against opposition and an auction for votes encouraged. If you are not part of the auction, you are in grave peril of being called either divisive or racist.

All of this at a time when the right thing to do is to prefer the national interest over the sectional interest.

The deregulation of the wheat industry represented a triumph of the national interest over the sectional interest. The deregulation of the rest of our economy, coastal shipping and the waterfront and most importantly, the labour market, can only happen if the sectional interest of the trade union movement gives way to the national interest.

This does not mean that the sectional interest should cease to exist, nor should it be denied some of its requests.

The point is that the good governance of Australia in the immediate future demands as never before a fixation on national goals and the national interest.

If multiculturalism is only about making people who choose Australia as their home feel welcome and guarantee they are given a fair go, then I am all for it.

If, however, as I suspect, it is another exercise in social engineering, its deficiencies should be trenchantly criticised.

*****

AUGUST 1989

Friday, 4 August 1989, p. 13

10

Howard's long-held interest in foreign policy issues sees him tackling the issue of sanctions arguing that the double standards of the Hawke Government had shown towards South Africa and China requires explanation.

'Why logic cannot sanction divisive double standards'

The Sino-Australian relationship which developed during the 1970's and 80's enjoyed bipartisan support.

Likewise, the loathing felt in Australia towards the recent tragic events in China spread equally across party lines.

The Hawke government's response to these sad events has not only been right, but has captured the mood of all shades of opinion in Australia.

The understandable display of distaste and anger at the cruel, indiscriminate suppression of a peaceful demonstration for greater freedom has been matched by the very sensible decision ruling out economic sanctions against China.

However, examining the reasons given by the Prime Minister and Senator Evans for not imposing sanctions on the Chinese produces some intriguing, indeed fascinating, explanations.

Whilst fully correct in themselves and entirely justified in the case of China, they reveal yet again the naked double standards adopted by many who support economic sanctions against South Africa.

No-one suggests for a moment that the refusal of the Hawke government to apply economic sanctions against China evinces any sympathy on its part for the Deng regime in Beijing.

In no way does it lend any support or credibility to the Goebbels-style explanations of what happened in June which now pour forth from Chinese embassies all around the world.

By not imposing economic sanctions the government cannot be accused in any way of condoning what the Chinese government did. Nor has it diminished its criticism of the cruel annihilation of those Chinese idealists who dared to hope that the economic freedom so assiduously encouraged by the very regime which then murdered them might have been matched by a scant amount of political freedom.

To my knowledge there has been no serious agitation in Australia for economic sanctions against China.

Not even the most strident and long-standing critics of the People's Republic have suggested there is any point in resorting to economic sanctions. This includes those who have shown over the years a complete disdain for the high priority given by governments from both sides to the development of the Chinese relationship.

There has been a sophisticated willingness to view the sanctions issue quite distinctly from our moral repugnance at the slaughter in Tiananmen Square.

Yet that very intelligence and maturity of judgement totally deserts the government and others in relation to anyone who criticises economic sanctions against South Africa.

There are many in Australia who intensely despise the system of apartheid but who genuinely believe economic sanctions against South Africa are counterproductive.

The stock response of the Hawke government is to brand these people as soft on apartheid. There is even a hint on occasions that such people harbour a secret admiration for some of the Afrikaner theories on racism.

This stark double standard is hard to fathom.

In terms of relative morality, it cannot seriously be argued that the South African regime is more abhorrent than the Beijing butchers.

It might be put by some that we should apply economic sanctions against South Africa so as to impress opinion in some Asian countries who have a particular revulsion towards South Africa.

On the grounds of proven national self-interest, that might be a sustainable argument if all those countries were themselves utterly consistent in their attitudes towards South Africa.

The same might be said of the front-line African states who maintain a level of commercial exchange with South Africa far beyond what they publicly require of other countries.

'Sophistication on China is missing on South Africa'

The other well-worn argument is that economic sanctions will induce change in South Africa.

That is probably true but it is not necessarily the change sought by those who support economic sanctions.

There is much evidence that poorer white South Africans have drifted from the National Party towards the far right wing Conservative Party in response to some of the economic changes and belt tightening brought about through economic sanctions.

Feeling their socio-economic position further squeezed, they have sought a solution in an even tougher imposition of apartheid.

It may not be logical but it has been an almost routine reaction of similar socio-economic groups all through history.

The supporters of economic sanctions naturally dismiss with total arrogance those within South Africa who oppose sanctions.

Bishop Tutu[25] and the ANC support sanctions. Their reasons may be totally bona fide.

---

[25] The Most Reverend Bishop Desmond Tutu, Archbishop of Cape Town, 1986-1996.

By contrast, Chief Buthelezi[26] of the Zulus, moderate white politicians such as Helen Suzman[27], corporate magnates such as Gavin Reilley of the giant Anglo-American Corporation and many others who are demonstrably not hard-line Afrikaners totally reject economic sanctions.

Their arguments are a mixture of concern that economic sanctions hurt blacks more than anyone else and a general view verified by the Rhodesian experience that economic sanctions provoke a spirit of national defiance which unites rather than divide the community.

When the sanctions argument warmed up several years ago, Helen Suzman argued:

> Nobody really gains in the long run by wrecking the economy of a country ... these things must be thought out very carefully because of the effects they have not only on South Africa and not only on the white electorate of South Africa but on the black population living here and in neighbouring (black) states.

Wherever the truth lies exactly it does seem clear that in common with other sanctions exercises this century those being applied against South Africa are unlikely to bring about decisive change for the better within that country.

Ironically the best possible argument against the use of economic sanctions in relation to South Africa has been provided by Senator Evans himself.

On July 13, announcing the government's ongoing policy towards China he said:

> Consistent with the government's desire to keep open lines of communication and maintain contacts at all possible

[26] The Honourable Mangosuthu Buthelezi MP, President, Inkatha Freedom Party, 21 March 1975 – 25 August 2019.

[27] South Africa Member of Parliament for Houghton, Johannesburg, 21 March 1975 – 25 August 2019.

> levels with the Chinese community, the government has decided against any other cuts to the aid program or any limits on cultural, economic and student exchanges. To do otherwise would not only involve closing rather than opening doors but would require the Chinese people to shoulder the burden of the conduct of their leaders.

In properly and logically disavowing sanctions against China he argued that we had to keep open channels of communication with the Chinese no matter how repelled Australia had been by the June massacre in Beijing.

He wisely looked beyond our present distaste for the Chinese regime to a better and more democratic future in that country.

The pointed claim in the Evans statement that if economic sanctions were imposed the Chinese people would be forced to carry the can for the conduct of their despised leaders is precisely the argument used several years ago by Margaret Thatcher and others regarding economic sanctions against South Africa.

Alone amongst Commonwealth leaders then she opposed economic sanctions despite threatened boycotts of the Commonwealth Games and stupid threats to even expel Britain from the Commonwealth.

Although he did not back British expulsion, Mr Hawke joined the anti-British chorus.

The Thatcher argument and that of many others who argued with her was exactly in line with the Evans Chinese doctrine. Sanctions would hurt the very people you wanted to help.

No-one has been left in any doubt about how strongly the Hawke government feels regarding recent events in China despite the fact that we are not imposing economic sanctions.

Surely the same attitude can in future be taken in relation to South Africa.

Is it not possible for people to oppose sanctions against South Africa without being openly accused of closet affection for apartheid?

Senator Evans' irrefutable logic regarding China should apply with equal force to South Africa.

*****

Friday, 11 August 1989, p. 13

11

The heroic status of Allan Border, who led the Australian cricket team to an Ashes revival victory in August 1989 at Old Trafford, is the focus of this week's column. Howard reflects on the nature of sportsmanship and underlines his love of the game of cricket. The six-test series beginning in June saw Australia win 4-0, only using 12 players for the whole series. Australia won the Ashes for the first time since 1982-83.

'A sportsman bordering on true greatness'

I know it is sacrilegious – in a sporting sense – to commence a tribute to Allan Border[28] with a reference to one of the great American baseball players.

But when Allan Border led his team to cricket fame two weeks ago I was put in mind of that Simon and Garfunkel lament of the late 1960s, 'where have you gone Joe DiMaggio? Our nation turns its lonely eyes to you'.

In a way the search for a straightforward, total sporting hero about which Simon and Garfunkel intoned seemed to me very apt for Allan Border.

This column is in praise of Allan Border – not for the most obvious reason that he led the Australian Cricket Team in regaining the Ashes on English soil for the first time in 55 years or because he has become one of the truly prolific run-getters in Australia's test cricket history.

---

[28] Allan Border AO began his Test career for Australia in the 1978-79 season against England, debuting at the Melbourne Cricket Ground. He would go on to play 156 Tests, including as captain for 93 consecutive Tests. Border ended his career by leading the first Australian team to play a Test series against South Africa in 1994. He is an original inductee of the International Cricket Committee Cricket Hall of Fame.

In themselves these are worthy reasons for the many accolades heaped on his shoulders over the past two weeks.

Above that Allan Border deserves our praise and gratitude because he is a stunning reminder of what Australian sportsmanship was always supposed to be about.

Despite the latter day lionisation of the 'knock 'em down', smash their teeth, murder em' philosophy of Australian sport not only viewed from time to time on television but practised fairly regularly by some parents on the sidelines Saturday morning football, Allan Border has reminded all of us that true sportsmanship is a combination of winning and grace.

He has reminded us that we can be proud of our sporting heroes even if they don't always 'win one for Australia'.

He has gone through the rough times, tasted defeat, faced up to the pressure and displayed great resilience. At the end of this he has won and won well and of course winning well is arguably as important as losing well.

Border's magnanimous remarks about David Gower and his instinctive modesty in recalling the valleys of despair through which he himself passed on the long march to his treasured moment of triumph at Old Trafford two weeks ago are the hallmarks of a true sportsman.

They also mark him as a man who not only understands the supreme imperative of winning in competitive sport but also the equally high calling of preserving the better values of a game – cricket – so indelibly part of our national psyche.

We tell our children of the need for dogged perseverance. All the old cliches about trying again, if at first you don't succeed, come to mind.

To have a prime living example of that in Allan Border is a real parental bonus.

It would have been so easy for him to have lapsed into oafish gloating. After all, he had seen off in his time several English captains and mastered all of their bowlers.

He had received a fearful bucketing from the now discredited Fleet Street sportswriters when he and his men arrived in England.

Many were foolish enough to call the team the worst side Australia had sent to England since World War II.

Through his difficult years as Australian captain he has suffered many indignities including a gratuitous piece of abuse from the current Prime Minister who, when the team was doing very poorly, called it a 'national disgrace'.

When I read of Border's generous comments regarding David Gower I was reminded of a recent statement by Sir Donald Bradman,

> When considering the stature of an athlete, or for that matter any person, I set great store on certain qualities which I believe to be essential in addition to skill.
>
> **'Combination of courage and modesty'**
>
> They are that the person conducts his or her life with dignity, with integrity, with courage and perhaps most of all with modesty. These virtues are totally compatible with pride, ambition and competitiveness'.

I can think of few Australian sportsmen in recent years who more accurately fit that description than Allan Border.

He has combined skill, success and monumental achievement with the maintenance of a degree of courage, tenacity and modesty. To these he has added magnanimity in victory.

All of it done in an unpretentious and direct manner.

In the many interviews given in his long career Allan Border has never been anything other than totally authentic and convincing.

When he's been in the miseries that has shown and when he spoke feelingly of David Gower, he clearly meant it.

He assumed the captaincy unexpectedly from Kim Hughes in 1984.

Through some incredibly bad patches and against enormous criticism and ridicule he has not only emerged triumphant as a captain, he has maintained his own exceptional performance as a batsman.

His greatest success over those years has been the response he has evoked from his own players. His determination and commitment has heartened them.

The partnership he has forged with Bob Simpson has played a major part in our cricket revival.

Simpson's own example of returning to the fray after the World Series cricket had decimated official Test cricket ranks in the 1970s merits its own eulogy.

As I reflected on the achievements of Allan Border and Bob Simpson, I recalled a Cabinet discussion during the Fraser government.

We had decided to spend more money on sport and the debate was all about where it would be spent.

The general push was to put almost all of the extra funds into those areas which would train and help the high achievers. There wasn't a lot earmarked for community sporting groups.

A few queried this and one of my former colleagues retorted 'sport in Australia is all about winning'.

In one sense he was right because at the time there was widespread concern that as a nation, we weren't supporting our best athletes as well as we might.

Indeed, the initiatives that came out of that discussion have proved of lasting benefit to Australian sport.

However, in a broader sense sport isn't only about winning.

The current drugs in sport drama is a prize example of the win at any cost mentality carried to its logical conclusion.

I can think of few sporting episodes more likely to induce cynicism amongst the young about the virtues of sport than the drug issue.

How good it is then to have in Allan Border someone who has demonstrably not sought to win at any cost – but has nonetheless made it and brought great credit to Australia.

Allan Border's success does more than restore faith in Australia's cricket ability.

It also restores the faith of many who do not believe that violent personal hatred and vitriol towards one's opponents both on and off the field is a necessary ingredient of sporting success. There are many in the community who do not believe one must hate in order to win.

Not only does his demeanour towards David Gower show this but he is known over the years to have had a close personal friendship with the English enfant terrible, Ian Botham.

As a batsman Border is a model of patient application, great consistency and all-round ability.

There is a lot of the quiet hero about him.

We haven't had many of them lately. We've had plenty of the noisy variety whose star soars for a while and then comes crashing down.

Perhaps in the age of instant television messages, the noisy ones grab our attention more readily.

In the longer run it's the quiet, consistent achievement of people like Allan Border who do more to build national pride.

His success challenges some of the prevailing cynicism of our time – so many people really thought he'd never make it. He and his team had been written off so often.

So much about Australia these days invokes cynicism. We need heroes and we need from time to time to beat cynicism or Australia will not have much of a future.

One way of doing this is simply to let the spotlight pause for a while on those sportsmen and women who display grace under pressure – and then go on to win continuing to show grace.

Allan Border is such a person.

*****

Friday, 18 August 1989, p. 11

12

Placing the national interest ahead of special interest groups is the key to good government, argues Howard. Drawing inspiration from his UK political ally, Prime Minister Margaret Thatcher, Howard challenges the Hawke Government to look past the entrenched privileges of the trade unions in tackling 'rigidities and weaknesses inherent in the Australian economy' currently protecting poor productivity.

'What about the world's greatest union statement?'

A few weeks ago we had the world's greatest environmental statement. Then we had the world's greatest multicultural statement. Apparently next week we are to witness the world's greatest sporting statement.

But there are some who regard this week's budget as being nothing other than the world's greatest retirement incomes statement.

We can expect many similar presentations between now and the next election. The pattern is only too familiar.

The government's PR machine produces an enormous amount of hype. The leading spokesmen for the interest group in question are regularly stroked weeks in advance to anticipate receiving every single morsel of all the ambit claims ever made on behalf of the interest group.

When the great day arrives the Prime Minister, complete with relevant portfolio Ministers, is paraded as an authentic, born-again environmentalist, multiculturalist, or whatever may be the case.

None of this is to deny the fact that statements targeting specific issues and specific interest groups are in themselves always bad or wrong.

Good government demands on occasions that kind of approach.

The great problem I see in today's economic climate is that this kind of approach is teaching us bad habits at precisely the wrong time in our economic history.

The world's greatest statement approach is a crude incentive for every sectional interest group in the community to go back to sectional interest politics, to eschew a broader national approach and to believe that if you talk loudly enough and long enough about your particular gripe or point of view, then ultimately the government will listen and come to the party with both money and policies.

Good government now and in the immediate future demands that sectional interests take second place to the national interest.

Many of the rigidities and weaknesses inherent in the Australian economy are the product of years of sectional interests triumphing over the national interest.

The long process of unwinding tariff protection demonstrates the extent to which sectional interests have become embedded in the national economy.

Economists constantly talk about structural adjustment.

So much of the structural adjustment required for the Australian economy, when reduced to bare essentials, involves removing some special arrangement or privilege, granted by government in response to a pressure group.

Many of the decisions involved were taken for the most benign reasons.

For decades the conventional wisdom about the Australian economy was that because of our size and particular circumstances in the world economy, different and usually highly protective arrangements were required to shield our tiny economy from the buffeting of an unfriendly world.

It has only been in more recent times that a new consensus has emerged recognising that such practices stunted our economic growth and increased our isolation from the rest of the world.

The most famous of all special deals is of course enshrined in our conciliation and arbitration system.

There is no more naked special deal than our arbitration system and its latter day manifestation of the prices and incomes accord.

This area highlights the great dilemma of the Hawke government.

On the one hand, it knows full well that in the name of economic sanity and economic rationalism it must reject special pleading and go to the national good.

It finally did this over Sydney airport. It was painfully late – six years late.

It presumably did this in relation to the frigate contract where despite enormous political pressure, it took a decision to award the contract to Williamtown based on a price advantage of some $300 million.

Yet on the other hand, it continues to walk away from any major micro economic reforms which touch upon the privileged position of the trade union movement.

The new Industry Commission may sound impressive. It's real service to the government will be to provide a political excuse (so the government hopes) to do nothing more on the micro front between now and the next election.

One of the real achievements of Margaret Thatcher has been to turn her face against special interest groups in Britain where she believes their demands or entrenched privileges are not in the national interest.

The most celebrated has been her historic breaking of the unjustified power of the trade union movement.

Less publicised, but no less important, has been her willingness to tackle perceived monopoly positions of groups such as lawyers.

In this respect she is seen in stark contrast to the Australian Prime Minister.

In Mrs Thatcher's case she not only tackles her political opponent's constituency, i.e. the trade union movement, but is also willing to take on a group, viz lawyers, who are normally amongst the most conservative in the community. Just ask the visiting Lord Chancellor of the United Kingdom[29] what that means.

It's always so easy to point the finger at the other fellow and tell him to deregulate his constituency. It gets a lot harder when you have to say no to those with whom one mingles in club or pub.

*****

[29] The Right Honourable James Mackay, 28 October 1987 – 2 May 1997.

Friday, 25 August 1989, p. 11

13

With Australian Federal Police Assistant Commissioner Colin Winchester assassinated in January in a suburban driveway in Canberra, Howard continues his fight against illegal drugs. Drawing parallels with the Colombian nightmare, Howard contends a growing cynicism is evident among the public about the effectiveness of the federal and state governments in dealing with the growing menace of organised crime in Australia.

'In the shadow of the needle and the gun'

If you think Australia has a drug problem spare a thought for Colombia.

A few days ago, the leading Presidential candidate, Louis Carlos Galan, was gunned down as he tried to address a political rally. He was strongly opposed to Colombia's drug bosses. His assassins belonged to a hit squad employed by one of the drug barons.

Colombia is the source of about 80 per cent of the cocaine imports into the United States. The major drug barons of Colombia employ private armies, the members of which have been expertly trained by mercenaries from all around the world.

The Colombian government is now supposedly engaged in a major crackdown although there are many who are cynical that the government is only going through the motions.

This has provoked an understandable response from the United States' Attorney-General who raised the prospect of US troops helping the Colombian authorities to rout the drug barons.

That may sound belligerent but when one contemplates the incredible social and human damage done to the youth of the United States by the massive importation of cocaine from countries such as Colombia, then it is seen in better perspective.

The grip of the drug barons in countries such as Colombia is so complete and their trade so insidious that its impact on the United States can easily be likened to war. Its long term effect is just as great.

The tragedy of Colombia is a good illustration of a country in a very advanced state of decay through the unrestricted growth of organised crime.

Assassination of police, politicians and members of the magistracy and the judiciary have become commonplace in those countries where organised crime has assumed the proportions of almost perpetual insurrection against the legally constituted government.

We may think these events are a millennium from Australia.

It cannot be suggested that this state of chronic instability and chaos is remotely similar to conditions now obtaining in Australia.

But we should not be so smug, complacent and superior as to think we couldn't get much closer to the Colombian nightmare than we would find comfortable.

Judges have been murdered in Australia.

All Australians must feel enormous trepidation and unease that the second highest ranking police officer in the Australian Capital Territory (ACT) should have been murdered in cold blood in his own driveway.

Organised crime in our country is a virulent threat not only to our children but to the way of life and peace of mind we have traditionally taken for granted as Australians.

At the end of last year when I launched 'Future Directions' on behalf of the opposition, there were sniggers from the cynics when I lamented that it was no longer possible in Australia to sleep with the door open on a hot night.

That may indeed be an impossible dream in urban Australia in 1989, however, there is deep resentment in the Australian community that much of the freedom from organised crime, once assumed to be part and parcel of Australian life, has disappeared in such a short space of time.

There is a sense of unease about the adequacy of government responses to organised crime. There is within our community a profound belief that in less than a generation the kind of society in which we now live has changed dramatically to a more vulnerable, less secure, more violent way of life.

Urgency

It seems to many that this issue does not occupy the central position in national political debate which its relevance and urgency demands.

For example, in typical Australian fashion political debate about the National Crime Authority revolves more around its alleged encroachment on States' rights than it does on its effectiveness in fighting organised crime.

Fierce rivalries between federal and state law enforcement agencies persist, yet despite these things, there is a dreadful paucity of national political debate about the overall threat which crime poses to our society.

A recent in-depth survey published by the Clemenger advertising agency starkly exposed growing community concern about crime related issues.

Entitled 'The Silent Majority II' the survey follows a similar one conducted twelve years ago.

It contains findings about the problems and concerns that adult Australians faced in their everyday lives.

'The Silent Majority II' survey replicated 1977 research. Its findings were illuminating and demonstrated very clearly that over the past 12 years there had been a dramatic upsurge in concern by average Australians about crime and related issues.

To quote from the survey itself it found that 'Australians are extremely worried about illegal drugs and increased crime in general and they are gravely concerned about the safety and future of their children'.

These concerns headed the list of a very exhaustive and in-depth survey.

It illustrated very sharply that crime and matters of physical and property security were in the forefront of the concerns of Australians.

The survey also recorded growing disenchantment with political leaders and public servants and it clearly emerged that in 1988 respondents were far more concerned about serious social issues than they were in 1977 when their concerns tended to focus more on immediate hip-pocket irritations.

There were some wild card results. AIDS for example did not reach the top 40 problems.

Some of the more radical feminists would be depressed to know that according to the survey women rank the portrayal of women in advertising 110th out of 187 problems – behind newspaper, ink on clothing, wax on apples and poor television over Christmas.

The typical responses of people who were expressing resentment about the failure and lack of confidence in the ability or willingness of authorities to deal with crime problems went as follows:

> They catch the little pawns, never the ones that control it – the big ones. The big guys protect at the expense of the little guy. It's the question – are the ones meant to protect us really dealers or what?

Such responses display not only deep-seated unease but a growing cynicism about the effectiveness of the system be it federal or state to deal with the growing menace of organised crime.

It is true, as the Clemenger survey acknowledges, that some of the heightened awareness is a direct product of greater media, particularly television, focus on violent crime. It is also a lamentable fact that in the 12 years since the previous survey many more have been directly touched by crime. It is either the house break-in or more sadly a child dying from a heroin overdose.

In the face of surveys such as the Clemenger one and other evidence of a growing community concern about the challenge to our society posed by organised crime, it is surprising this issue does not bulk larger in national political debate.

Without in any way being facetious, I suggest to the Prime Minister that he would win a good deal more respect and recognition from the Australian public if he were to turn his mind over coming months to producing the world's greatest statement on fighting organised crime. In doing this he would not be buttering up small pressure groups but listening to the silent majority.

A lot has been done and I do not wish to denigrate the Greiner government's ICAC nor indeed the courageous work of the Fitzgerald Inquiry in Queensland.

Nevertheless, there is an absence of national focus.

I do not argue that the national government should seek to occupy the entire field. Perish the thought.

If the future protection of our physical environment is important enough to provoke the involvement of our national government, then so is our simple desire that our children and the elderly travel and live their lives without unreasonable fear of molestation.

Far away Colombia is a world apart from Australia but there is a lesson in her tragic anarchy which all of us would do well to learn.

There is not the slightest doubt that within Australia there are adequate number of criminals who would readily emulate the amorality and truculence of Colombia's crime bosses.

Over time all they need is a complacent population and an adequate government response.

*****

SEPTEMBER 1989

Friday, 1 September 1989, p. 13

14

Given Prime Minister Bob Hawke is backing both the ACTU and the airlines against the pilots in a protracted pay dispute, Howard proposes a market-based approach to resolve the issue. With the Australian Federation of Air Pilots seeking a 30 per cent pay rise for its members, the dispute involved pilots, domestic airlines, and the federal government, including armed forces flying commercial routes. Howard was adamant negotiated productivity improvements were central to resolving the dispute. The pilots' dispute is one of Australia's most expensive and protracted industrial disputes, costing an estimated billion dollars.

'Pilots' dispute may yet to be productive'

Those of us who want a decentralised wages system must hope and pray that the airline pilots dump their union and strike direct deals with the airlines based on productivity improvements.

That outcome would do more than anything else to weaken the flawed, centralised wage fixation system and strike a blow for a freer market-based approach to industrial relations and wage fixation.

Ironically such a result would be almost exactly in line with how the Hawke Labor government now sees the dispute as being settled.

It is one of the bizarre ironies of this dispute that the Prime Minister is now advocating a course of action which, if followed, will do more to weaken his beloved centralised wage fixation system than almost any other possible method of settling the dispute.

The government has declared the pilots to be outside the system. The Pilots' Federation is now regarded as totally irrelevant by the government and the airlines. In the eyes of the government it is an industrial relations outlaw.

Every action and all the rhetoric of the Prime Minister and his ministers in recent days has been to encourage individual pilots to negotiate directly with the airlines.

In Parliament earlier this week Mr Willis[30] declared great satisfaction that several hundred pilots has responded to the direct advertisements of the airlines for pilots to fly their planes.

Does he not realise that this is the stuff of which a decentralised wage fixation system is made?

If in fact the strike is settled by pilots doing direct deals with the airlines, then not only will some of the pilots aim in the dispute have been achieved, but also a precedent will have been established for more and more groups in the community to do exactly the same thing.

I find it amazing that in a dispute declared by the government to be so critical to Australia's economic future this government should totally misunderstand the power dynamics not only of the dispute but also of its own centralised wage fixation system.

A centralised wage fixation system depends for its survival on the continued existence of strong and powerful unions.

Without powerful unions the centralised wage fixation system will weaken and, in time, disappear. It is built on union power.

It is the representation of large numbers of workers before a central tribunal and the capacity of those representatives viz. unions to win industrial relations gains in the field and pass those gains on to their members which underpins a centralised wage fixation system.

---

[30] The Honourable Ralph Willis AO, Labor Minister for Transport and Communications, 2 September 1988 – 4 April 1990 later Treasurer of Australia, 23 December 1993 – 11 March 1996.

'Direct deals would inflict a mortal wound on the centralised wage-fixing system'

The working capital of comparative wage justice is the assumption that one man's wage rise will be bludgeoned for all other men through the industrial clout exercised by powerful unions.

Therefore, any progress towards a decentralised system must involve a reduction in the power of trade unions.

This will take two forms.

First, it involves removing legal privileges from trade unions. That of course is a central element of the opposition's industrial relations policy.

Second, and importantly so far as the pilots' dispute is concerned, it will also involve the by-passing of unions in the working out of individual industrial relations disputes.

Pressure

The more disputes there are settled directly between employers and employees, the less relevant become not only trade unions but also industrial tribunals.

Direct bargains between employers and employees are the killing fields of a centralised industrial relations system.

The very essence of a decentralised system is to have direct negotiation at an enterprise level between owners of the enterprise and the workers in the enterprise.

In the case of the pilots' dispute this translates into direct agreements between the airlines and the pilots – without the intervention of the government, the industrial relations commission and most importantly, the Pilots' Federation itself.

The Pilots' Federation does not want direct deals. It knows that if these occur any bargain struck will have something in it for both parties.

In other words, if a wage increase is granted then a productivity improvement will need to be forthcoming in return.

With airlines deregulation coming next year there is no way any of the airlines will agree to a significant wage increase for pilots without extracting an adequate productivity offset in return.

Those who sneer at the operation of market forces in this dispute totally ignore the enormous market pressure that will be imposed upon the airlines by deregulation to ensure that their operations are lean and cost efficient.

It is therefore in the national economic interest that a deal be struck between individual pilots and the airlines. This will certainly pave the way for wage increases based on productivity improvements.

It is the right vehicle for ending an insanely crippling strike which is doing untold damage to our precious tourist industry as well as many other Australian industries.

A settlement in this fashion would inflict a mortal wound on the centralised wage fixation system.

This really appears to have totally escaped our Prime Minister who is more intent on peddling the absurdity that the opposition's industrial relations policy has in some way produced the strike.

Let that canard be put down for good.

It has been the iron law of Labor's accord which has ruled the industrial relations arena for the past six and a half years.

It is the government's inflexible, highly centralised, union dominated hidebound industrial relations system which has been unable to cope with this dispute.

Trapped

It is the Hawke government's commitment to centralised wage fixation and its manic opposition to enterprise-based agreements which spawned this strike in the first place.

Now, of course, we have the supreme irony of a Prime Minister who has dedicated most of his life to defending Australia's centralised industrial relations system trapped by his own extreme language into advocating a course of action which if followed, will in fact undermine the very system he has championed for decades.

As each day goes by more and more commentators proclaim the pilots' strike as some kind of watershed in Australia's industrial relations history.

Whether that turns out to be the case depends very much on when and how the dispute is settled.

If it is settled by the pilots meekly returning to the system, then nothing will have been gained and an enormous amount will have been lost.

The pilots by their wilful, and to many selfish conduct, will have done serious damage to the Australian economy.

For good measure their surrender back into the embrace of the industrial relations club will have further underwritten a system which is inimical to the long-term international competitiveness and productivity growth of our nation.

On the other hand, if the strike is settled by the pilots dumping their union and reaching agreements with the airlines based on pilots working harder and longer hours for higher pay then perhaps some of the acknowledged damage done to the economy by the strike can in the long run be balanced by the blow that would have been struck by such a settlement for a freer, enterprise based industrial relations system.

Every industrial relations dispute which enhances the status of agreements between people who work together as distinct from systems being imposed upon people who work together is a step towards a stronger, more competitive economy.

That means in practice the steady dismantling of union power and influence.

The government should know this (but has got in to such a tangle as to forget it in the current dispute). The ACTU certainly knows it, that is why many senior ACTU figures greet with trepidation the Prime Minister's behaviour in the dispute.

Let us therefore hope that the national interest triumphs and the strike ends soon through a productivity-based agreement between the pilots and the airlines without hide nor hair of either Captain McAuley and his cohorts in the Pilots' Federation or the mandarins of the industrial relations club.

*****

Friday, 8 September 1989, p. 13

15

With 'Watergate' exercising the imaginations of journalists and politicians in the United States and Australia, Howard tackles political corruption and cautions against disclosure of donations and a proposed ban on political advertising. Howard contends existing laws did not prevent 'Watergate' nor the corrupt behaviour of a serving US Vice President. With an anti-corruption body established in NSW, Howard fears that such laws will not make politicians more honest or foster a less corrupt political system. His preference being the personal honour and decency of men and women who serve in our political system - coupled with a free and vigorous media - to maintain an incorruptible political system in Canberra.

'Why the war on corruption is a matter of honour'

The word 'Watergate' is hurled around with reckless abandon by those in the Labor party, the media and elsewhere who zealously want to reform our electoral laws.

The argument is that Australia needs more draconian laws requiring the disclosure of donations to political parties and even prohibitions on political advertising to prevent the occurrence in Australia of a Watergate-style incident.

There is an enormous irony in this.

It is widely believed that the infamous Nixon 'enemies list' was in fact culled from the public record of contributions to the Democratic party required to be maintained under the political donations disclosure laws of the United States.

Furthermore, Nixon's own Vice President, Spiro Agnew[31], was

[31] 38th Vice President of the United States, 20 January 1969 – 10 October 1973.

found guilty of taking bribes in the executive building while serving as Vice President.

In other words, elaborate, complicated and seemingly strict disclosure laws did not prevent – in fact may have facilitated – events related to Watergate, let alone prevent the corruption of a former Vice President of the United States of America.

I have never accepted the arguments given for laws requiring the disclosure of political donations.

There is no evidence that such laws make politicians more honest or foster a less corrupt political system.

In my view such laws are the necessary political trade-off for raiding the taxpayers' pocket via public funding to pay for the election campaigns of political parties.

I have always inclined to the adage that if there is no instinct for honour in public life it cannot be legislated.

That point was regularly made by my former colleague, Sir James Killen[32], when he frequently inveighed against the pecuniary interest disclosure requirements urged upon the federal parliament by the Labor party some years ago.

Although I am genuinely cynical about the worth of compelling the public disclosure of political donations, I accept that such an attitude will be described as wishing to maintain the secrecy of the clandestine gifts of the rich and powerful, who hope to wield undue clout and influence.

Where is the evidence at a federal level in Australia to sustain the charge?

The presumption behind the existing disclosure laws and certainly the extensions now being proposed is that there is something corrupt about the federal political system.

I recognise what has been disclosed in Queensland and we all

[32] The Honourable Sir James Killen, AC. KCMG, Liberal Minister for Defence in the Fraser Government, 11 November 1975 – 7 May 1982.

wait to see what might be disclosed in New South Wales by the ICAC. Western Australia is also on our minds.

However, the fact is that to date, our federal political scene has been remarkably free of corruption. I include both sides of politics in that observation.

Federal politicians make fewer decisions affecting the immediate property, prosperity and profits of individuals. They are more preoccupied with broader national issues.

Moreover, the federal parliamentary press gallery maintains a more high profile and rigorous approach to the politicians they scrutinise than do their state counterparts.

Nonetheless, the bottom line is that Canberra has been to a remarkable extent corruption free.

It is therefore depressing as well as offensive that the government should act in a way which serves to underwrite the more cynical views in the community about our national political system, particularly when in relation to corruption that cynicism is utterly misplaced.

For example, the Joint Parliamentary Committee Report on Electoral Funding is entitled 'Who Pays the Piper Calls the Tune'.

The implication is that those who contribute to political parties at a federal level have undue influence.

Yet paradoxically, when the report is read there is an acknowledgement that the federal political process has not been stained by corruption.

I cannot speak for the Labor Party, and I make no allegations.

But having served as a senior minister for some years in a coalition administration, I saw no evidence of any favouritism in the more than seven years of the Fraser government which had an impeccable record on such matters.

We now operate under the 1984 disclosure laws of the Hawke

government which also ushered in public funding. The government appears certain to extend and strengthen those laws.

Thus far neither government spokesmen nor party apparatchiks have proffered any convincing evidence to justify the further invasions of privacy which will be involved in the quite extensive changes recommended in the Parliamentary Committee Report.

Yet the government now seems hellbent on amending the disclosure laws in a way that could only be appropriate if there were hard evidence of political favouritism or corruption.

'New laws will not make MPs more honest'

There are some basic issues of freedom involved here.

One of the Committee's suggestions is that there be full disclosure of all donations to political parties.

That is a direct threat to freedom of association. That freedom to have any meaning must include privacy of association.

For example, some single-issue parties champion very unpopular causes.

Is democracy really served by such parties being denied funds because potential donors are scared off by public disclosure laws?

The irresistible conclusion is that the proposals now doing the rounds and being enthusiastically endorsed by people such as Bob Hogg[33], the National Secretary of the ALP, are designed to give the Labor Party a political advantage.

It is no coincidence that a requirement for full disclosure has a much lighter impact on the trade union donor base of the Labor Party than it does on the Liberal and National parties.

We all know that the AMSWU kicks in to help Bob Hawke. There is no individual embarrassment involved here. Given the history of Australian politics it is hardly surprising that trade unions regularly support the Labor Party.

---

[33] Bob Hogg AO, Australian Labor Party National Secretary, 1988-1993.

However, the case of individual donations is quite different.

Surely Mrs Smith of Gladesville has the right to preserve the anonymity of her $100 donation to the Liberal party or indeed to the Labor party for that matter.

The zeal does not stop at disclosure laws.

Although its ardour may have cooled the Labor party was at one stage determined to erode the commercial freedom of television stations as well as the political rights of minor parties.

The Labor majority on the Joint Parliamentary Committee wanted to compel TV stations to provide free time in lieu of paid commercial advertising.

This would be a blatant confiscation of the assets of commercial enterprises.

If this has any legs left, then the networks should resist it to the hilt.

Moreover, the later and more general proposition that the paid advertising should be banned is totally indefensible.

If political advertising is boring, then the parties will suffer.

In any event, what right has the government to decree that putting a political message is inherently more against the public interest than encouraging people to drink liquor, savour breakfast cereal or swan it on Hamilton Island (if you can get a flight)?

It smacks of patronising paternalism.

There is a story that on one occasion, when Ben Chifley[34] was Prime Minister, he was handed a donation of one thousand pounds for the Labor Party.

The donor said, 'now let's talk policy', whereupon Chifley returned the money and said 'now we can talk about policy'.

Knowing the immense reputation for integrity deservedly enjoyed by the late Ben Chifley I am sure that story is true.

---

[34] The Right Honourable Ben Chifley, 16th Prime Minister of Australia, 13 July 1945 – 19 December 1949.

It says it all.

The true guarantees of an incorrupt political system are the personal honour and decency of men and women who comprise our political system coupled with a free and vigorous media.

*****

Friday, 15 September 1989, p. 11

16

A friend in need is a friend indeed. Howard continues his interest in foreign policy by sharing his admiration for a South African leading light, former Ambassador to Australia and co-leader of the Democratic Party, Dr Dennis Worrall. Critiquing the situation in South Africa and holding firm on the need for bipartisan support for change, Howard foregrounds the wave of reform that would ultimately envelope South Africa in 1994 - with the election of President Nelson Mandela.

'Glimmers of hope in whitest Africa'

About six years ago I had the pleasure to know Dr Dennis Worrall, then South African Ambassador in Canberra. He was an intelligent, decent man of genuine liberal instincts.

As his country's envoy to Australia, he grappled manfully with the daunting task of explaining and defending policies he clearly despised while maintaining a fierce commitment to the country he loved.

Dr Worrall left Australia to become Ambassador in London. He quit this post some years ago to enter South African politics.

Yesterday it pleased me to pen Dr Worrall a note of congratulations on his election as a Democratic party member of the South African parliament.

His victory is symbolic in that the outcome of the recent South African election provides some genuine hope that a catastrophe can be avoided in South Africa.

Limited though it was as a democratic exercise, the election was nonetheless an important test of white opinion.

The real victory in the election belongs to those within the white population in South Africa who, however tentatively and carefully, nonetheless favour reforms and some kind of partnership with the black and coloured majority in running the South Africa of the future.

Despite the wordy protestations to the contrary, the election was a great disappointment to the far-right Conservative Party.

For that we can all breathe a hefty sigh of relief.

Although the Conservative Party obtained about 31 per cent of the vote and increased the number of seats it previously held in the whites-only South African Parliament, it fell far short of the target it had set itself.

The Democratic (liberal) party gave the most spirited showing and for those who believe that the only hope for South Africa lies in dialogue between liberal whites and moderate blacks the performance of Mr Malan, Dr Worrall and their colleagues of the Democratic party was very heartening.

If one accepts, as is undoubtedly the case, that a growing group in the ruling National party has views approaching those of the Democratic Party it means that a sizeable chunk of the white population now recognises that their country has no future unless there is a fair and sensible accommodation with the black majority.

Significantly, Mr de Klerk[35] himself declared after the election that 70 per cent of the white population wanted reform.

That he feels sufficiently confident to align himself in the eyes of the white electorate with the Democratic party as distinct from the Conservative party is of itself an enormous step forward.

The great danger in the recent election was always that the liberals would be decimated, and the Conservative party would make massive gains at the expense of everyone else.

---

[35] His Excellency Fredrik Willem de Klerk OMG DMS, 7th State President of South Africa, 14 August 1989 – 10 May 1994.

Pre-election fears that boycotts and widespread unrest would scare white voters into the arms of the far Right fortunately proved largely groundless.

The election result has broken the historical pattern of white politics in South Africa.

In the past decisive re-alignments within the white electorate have normally been to the right.

The Nats won office in 1948 by placing themselves to the right of Jan Smuts' United party.

Smuts' United party had been formed to unite the English and Afrikaans speaking white South Africans.

The Nats had never wanted this amalgamation and exploited fears within the white electorate that the United party would not be zealous enough in maintaining white supremacy.

As the years passed each successive National party Prime Minister seemed more pro-apartheid than his predecessor.

When P.W. Botha[36] commenced a limited dilution of apartheid in the early 1980's he lost a large component of his party in the Transvaal. Under Dr Treurnicht they formed the Conservative party.

It then looked for all the world as though the historical pattern would be repeated.

Fears of this were borne out in the 1986 election when the Conservative party made great inroads into the National party vote. It became the official opposition.

For these reasons the relatively modest performance of the far-right conservatives in the recent election is of immense significance.

If they had continued their forward march then all hope of sanity in that unhappy country would have been lost.

---

[36] Pieter Willem Botha DMS, 6th State President of South Africa, 3 September 1984 – 14 August 1989.

None of these positive remarks are meant to suggest for a moment that a new dawn is about to come in South Africa.

'We must give credit, if due'

It is still a highly regimented, authoritarian country. Its apartheid creed is still utterly unacceptable to the rest of the world.

However, given the frequent predictions of Armageddon which have come forth regarding South Africa over recent years, any noticeable shift of opinion within the ruling white community is of great moment to those who genuinely want to see a peaceful multi-racial South Africa evolve in the future.

There have been hopeful signs since the election.

The decision of the government to officially sanction an anti-apartheid demonstration in Cape Town is probably without precedent.

No doubt it will be greeted with a cynical response from all sides but against the culture of recent years in South Africa it is a powerful symbol of the greater confidence the South Africa government now feels in taking steps towards liberating the system.

Of more than passing importance have been the vocal comments of a coloured police officer regarding the brutality of sections of the security forces.

That he should feel sufficient confidence to make his remarks in such a forthright way and that they should receive wide publicity is also a sign of cracks appearing in the previously tightly held security system.

De Klerk's reform agenda is vague. He clearly does not support and indeed cannot support one man-one vote.

He has made a general commitment to a federal structure in South Africa. Exactly how this would be achieved is left very much to conjecture.

The significant thing is that he is now, however haltingly, pointed down the path of accommodation with the black majority.

Clearly the release of Nelson Mandela[37] can only now be a matter of time.

The reaction of western countries, particularly those with great economic and political clout, is crucial.

They must walk a delicate line between the maintenance of sufficient pressure to propel the South African government further along the reform path without being so short-sighted as not to acknowledge when appropriate improvements for the better inside of South Africa.

However much the purists may be offended, the reality is that there will be no overnight transition to one man one vote within South Africa.

There must be a process of evolution but at a much faster pace than before. That can only be built on co-operation and understanding between liberal whites and moderate blacks.

If it is to be peaceful and constructive, South Africa's future lies with Dr Worrall and Chief Buthelezi rather than Dr Treurnicht of the Conservative party or the more radical leadership of the African National Congress.

If the only alternative given to the white population is a virtual immediate surrender of their current political and economic dominance, then they will stand and fight.

In the end they will probably lose but the victory the black majority might gain will not be worth having.

It will embrace a ruined economy, plummeting living standards as well as political chaos.

That is why an accommodation in the centre is so critical.

It must be an accommodation driven by the growing liberalism

---

37 His Excellency Nelson Mandela, 1st President of South Africa, 10 May 1994 – 14 June 1999.

within South Africa and the more pragmatic black leaders who fully understand that a somewhat less than totally democratic South Africa is not only infinitely better than the present situation but utterly preferable to the wreckage which will inevitably flow from any attempt at total revolution.

Something of a show-down looms between Mr de Klerk and his western creditors in the next 12 months.

He must go far enough along the path of reform to show he is utterly genuine.

They in return must not set the bar so high that the hardliners within South Africa, ever ready to argue that the West can never be satisfied, do not receive an undeserved boost to their cause.

A flicker of hope now burns in South Africa.

For it to grow in strength the de Klerk government will need to deliver and deliver fast on reforms. The rest of the world must be willing to give credit if and when it is due.

*****

Friday, 22 September 1989, p. 11

17

Advocating a lower tax burden for Australians, Howard continues his push for a fairer tax system. Decrying the Hawke Government's attempts at taxation reform and its budget measures failing to match its rhetoric, Howard plants the seed for privatisation and waterfront reform.

'Beware, pickpocket at work'

'More than half the workforce now pays a marginal tax rate almost one third higher than four years ago'

Remember the economy? If one were super-cynical it would be possible to believe that one of the reasons the Prime Minister has given enormous profile to the pilots' dispute is to divert attention from the economy.

So complete has been the domination of the news by the airlines issue that analytical coverage of developments with the economy over the past few weeks has virtually disappeared. At the very least it has gone off the front pages.

This has coincided with a quite ominous worsening of expectations regarding interest rates. These can only deteriorate further in the wake of yesterday's quite appalling current account deficit for August of $2.58 billion, the worst on record.

It is only a few weeks since both the Treasurer and the Prime Minister waxed lyrical about the beneficial impact of the $9 billion surplus on home loan interest rates.

We were all assured that they were coming down. Although the arrival at the hearth of the bacon was not promised again, we were given more than a wink and a nudge that come the end of the year most of us would be paying less for our housing loan.

The Prime Minister was adamant that interest rates would fall before the end of the year.

Even Bernie Fraser, then Treasury Secretary, joined the chorus.

However, more recently, this tune has changed.

At the recent EPAC meeting the Treasurer belled the cat on some of the previous very optimistic predictions.

It was, he told us, to be a long, hard road of high interest rates for some time. There were even stories that Labor party strategists were planning to be re-elected despite high interest rates.

Some of those stories about the greater sophistication of the electorate on economic issues also appeared with greater frequency.

And, of course, yesterday the National Bank lifted a few of its deposit rates this sparking real speculation that so far from home loan interest rates coming down they could well go up yet again before the end of the year.

The fact is that high interest rates are driven far more by the huge and continuing current account deficit and hence rising overseas debt than they are by the size of the budget surplus.

A surplus of $9 billion although better than $7 billion is increasingly a drop in the ocean when the Australian economy is staring at an annual current account deficit of $18 billion and a gross overseas debt of $140 billion.

It has been the growing acceptance of this in recent weeks, the realisation that the current account will get worse before it has any hope of getting better, and significantly the inevitable impact of the pilots' dispute on our tourist earnings which together have combined to turn around sentiment about interest rates.

On top of this there have employment, retail sales, and housing figures some of which go against the government's publicly stated belief that the high interest rate regime of recent months would bring the bucking bronco to heel.

The markets are clearly saying that until a believable strategy to reduce the current account deficit over a foreseeable time frame and to keep it within manageable limits is produced, they are simply not going to validate reductions in interest rates.

As many commentators pointed out, the budget, despite its commendable initiatives in the superannuation area simply failed to deliver the goods on micro-economic reform.

The Hawke government has had several opportunities to parade its efficiency wares on issues such as the waterfront and coastal shipping. On each instance it has failed.

I am sure the great majority of Australians would welcome direct employer-employee contracts on the waterfront.

Why can't the line taken by the Prime Minister on the pilots be applied to the wharves? Oh no! We are told 'industrial realities prevent that happening'.

The pathetic retreat of John Kerin[38] in the face of the Wheat Board's (since abandoned) proposals to bypass the Waterside Workers' Federation showed clearly that the Hawke government has little stomach for a fight on the waterfront.

Very recently we have received strong signs that it will not bite the bullet on the issue of privatisation.

Apparently, we are to be treated to some convoluted financing techniques which will procure for enterprises such as Qantas some private sector money which is neither straight debt nor straight equity.

That this government is now reduced to contortions of this kind is another stark illustration that it really has lost any reformist zeal it might have had in the micro-economic area.

Then of course we could turn to taxation.

On this score I am indebted to an excellent paper produced by

---

[38] The Honourable John Kerin AO, Labor Minister for Primary Industries and Energy, 11 March 1983 – 3 June 1991 later Treasurer of Australia, 4 June 1991 – 8 December 1991.

Sir William Cole now of the Australian Institute of Public Policy, formerly head of the Department of Finance, the Public Service Board, and Secretary of the Department of Defence.

Entitled 'A Tax System for the 1990s' it canvasses some eminently sensible reforms of the taxation system.

However, it unearths a fascinating statistic of which this writer and I suspect many others were not previously conscious.

Unbelievable though it may be and despite the so called tax reforms of April last, which of course followed the so called tax reforms some three years earlier, a person on only 80 per cent of average weekly earnings is now on a marginal tax rate which is almost one third higher than the same person's marginal tax rate in 1985.

Battler

The figures are 39 cents in the dollar compared with 30 cents in the dollar. When it is borne in mind that median weekly earnings are 91 per cent of AWE then it is obvious that more than half of the entire Australian workforce now pays a marginal tax rate almost one third higher than was the case four years ago.

One does not need to be an economic genius to deduce that a package of tax reforms which has seen the jacking up from 30 to 39 per cent of the marginal tax rate for the majority of personal tax payers can hardly dignify itself with the description of a real taxation reform.

In his excellent paper, Sir William recalls the Treasurer's rhetoric about high rates of marginal tax in the government's white paper of 1985.

In that paper, Mr Keating quite correctly points out that the top rate of tax then applied at only one and a half times average weekly earnings, whereas in the 1950s and '60s it did not begin to bite until a taxpayer was enjoying something like seven to ten times average weekly earnings if not indeed more in the mid- '50s.

None of this is to suggest that high rates of marginal tax have only existed during the lifetime of the Hawke government.

However, the point must be made that despite six years of government and two loudly trumpeted efforts at taxation reform, the average Aussie battler in 1989 is in fact paying a higher rate of tax at the margin of his income than he was in 1985 let alone the position which obtained in 1983.

The pilots' dispute has engulfed the political news over the past month. That is barely surprising. The dispute is enormously costly to the Australian economy.

Our industrial relations will never be the same again.

As I have observed on other occasions, the Hawke government by its deeds is facilitating a change in our industrial relations system which owes more to the philosophy of the Liberal and National parties' industrial relations policy than it does to the icons of the accord.

It is hard to know whether this strategy is deliberate or unwitting or perhaps a combination of both.

Whatever the prime ministerial intent our gaze has in the process been turned from the more mundane but ongoing features of the economy.

During this time in two areas at least, which affect all of us, interest rates and taxation, a closer more sober analysis would not have been something which the government would have found at all comfortable.

*****

Friday, 29 September 1989, p. 11

18

With the pilots' dispute entering its sixth week, Howard voices his support for small business operators impacted by protracted action but insists capitulating to the pilots on unfavourable terms is not in the national interest.

'Let's salvage something'

The pilots' dispute has taken an enormous toll. By far the worst hit have been the innocent bystanders running small businesses in tourism, catering and entertainment.

It is a very cruel irony that these industries are amongst the least unionised in Australia yet are being more painfully treated than any others through the failure of our current industrial relations system.

The longer the dispute drags on, the greater becomes the pressure for it to be settled – almost at any cost.

Over the past week a growing number of voices have cried, 'Enough is enough, get it settled no matter how'. This is understandable but misguided.

The worst possible outcome is for the dispute to be settled in a way that does not improve our industrial relations system.

Despite the enormous cost nothing will have been achieved if the dispute is ended in a way that ratifies and entrenches the worst features of the very industrial relations system that produced the dispute in the first place.

Yet we may well be on the verge of such a settlement.

I greet with no joy at all the intervention of the Industrial Relations Commission. It is strange that some should throw their hats in the air regarding the so-called Maddern initiative.

Perhaps the dispute has now gone on for so long and has involved so many role reversals that many people have lost sight of the principles at stake.

The worst possible outcome would be one which combined a healthy wage hike for the pilots in return for little gain in productivity.

This is far more likely to occur within the embrace of the Industrial Relations Commission than otherwise.

There is little doubt that if the airlines continue down the path of direct negotiation with individual pilots the result will be significant wage rises based on major productivity gains.

That, of course, is the logical outworking of a freer, more market sensitive wages system. It does no economic harm; indeed, yields an economic benefit. It is also, incidentally, squarely in line with the Industrial Relations Policy of the Liberal and National Parties.

There is a market imperative called deregulation which will ensure that the airlines do not yield wage rises without obtaining productivity improvements.

Once the issue comes back to the Commission, where the parties can only be the airlines and the Australian Federation of Air Pilots, that same market imperative must compete with other pressures and will not play the same dominant role in the ultimate settlement of the dispute.

These include the overwhelming pressure to find a settlement, to compromise, to allow both parties to save face and above all, of course, to preserve the centralised wage fixation system.

'The worst outcome is for the dispute to be settled in a way that doesn't better our industrial relations system'

Thrown into the cauldron all at once, these pressures are infinitely more likely to deliver an outcome which involves a pretty substantial wage rise in return for a fairly bogus productivity improvement.

Apart from anything else, there is the little matter of one of the restructuring principles not allowing any staff redundancies if productivity improvements are obtained. Put bluntly the Industrial Relations Commission is not going to agree to fewer pilots being employed as part of any settlement it blesses.

That very barrier alone makes it almost impossible to conceive that any productivity improvements under an arrangement worked out before, and sanctioned by, the Industrial Relations Commission could possibly match the productivity gains that would result from a direct bargain between the airlines and individual pilots.

This dispute has been very costly. That is all the more reason to salvage something by way of a permanent change in our industrial relations culture out of the difficulty and turmoil of the past six weeks.

Any of those wanting major changes to our industrial relations system who believe it can be achieved without difficulty and some temporary costs are living in fairyland.

The landmark disputes in Britain and the United States such as the miners', Wapping, and the air traffic controllers all involved dislocation but each in its different way played a part in changing the rules of the industrial game in those countries.

They also produced enormous attitudinal changes.

Where would industrial relations in Britain be today if an industrial relations compromise had been forced on the News Corporation management and the printing unions at Wapping? Where indeed would be the current higher level of efficiency and productivity in the British news media?

The same rhetorical question would produce a like answer in relation to the air traffic controllers dispute in the United States.

It is therefore blindingly obvious that if nothing at all changes as a result of the pilots' dispute, it will go down in Australian history as one of the most costly, wasteful and unproductive disputes ever.

It would confirm the views of the pessimists who believe we have an almost manic incapacity to turn around the industrial culture in this country.

Nothing which has happened in recent weeks alters the plain unassailable fact that an outcome based on direct contracts between the airlines and individual pilots will do more than any other outcome to weaken the centralised wage fixation system.

Given the view I and many others hold that breaking down that system is in Australia's long term economic interests because it is the only way we can ever hope to have a wage fixing system truly based on productivity, then I continue to hope that the dispute is ultimately resolved in that manner.

It remains one of the supreme ironies of this dispute that both the Prime Minister and leadership of the ACTU has behaved, for a large part of the dispute, in a way that wittingly or otherwise was facilitating the industrial relations policy of the Liberal Party.

They have not had this objective in mind. They have naively thought the pilots could be a one-off case.

They have rested their case for isolating and by-passing a union viz the Australian Federation of Air Pilots on the proposition that the Federation has gone outside the system and is not in any event an affiliate of the ACTU.

In terms of protecting their beloved centralised wage fixing system these are flimsy specious distinctions.

If after the dust has settled and the Federation has been successfully by-passed by the airlines signing up enough pilots to become fully operational such distinctions will be of little to no account.

The centralised system will have been dealt a very heavy blow. Industrial relations in Australia will never be the same again.

Therein of course lies the real significance of Barry Maddern's intervention. He knows that direct contracts between employers and individual employees will undermine the centralised wage fixation system. He has sensed the enormous threat posed to the dominant role of the Industrial Relations Commission by resolution of the pilots' dispute based on the airlines ultimately signing up enough pilots to restore the full operational capacity of their companies.

In convening the special conference this week, the President of the Commission was acting as much to preserve the present system as he was to resolve the dispute. That is not an unduly cynical view because those who run our centralised wage fixing system devoutly believe it to be in the national economic interest.

There is no greater sin before the industrial relations club than undermining 'the system'.

The unreality of our present industrial relations system was really epitomised by Mr Justice Maddern's request to the parties to refrain from public comment.

I assume this request was limited to the airlines and the Pilots' Federation. If it extended to the Government, then its arrogance was truly breathtaking.

It is yet another example of the Commission behaving in an over-legalistic fashion. He may be styled a judge, but the President of the Commission does not exercise judicial functions.

Furthermore, both the airlines and the Pilots' Federation have a totally legitimate right to advocate their point of view and inform the public about the dispute at all times. The suggestion that in some way the Commission knows best is yet another case of 'the system' taking itself too seriously.

On 1 September I wrote in this column,

> … if the strike is settled by the pilots dumping their union and reaching agreements within the airlines based on pi-

> lots working harder and longer hours for higher pay, then perhaps some of the acknowledged damage done to the economy by the strike can … be balanced by the blow that would have been struck by such a settlement for a freer enterprise-based industrial relations system.

My view has not altered. The longer the dispute lasts the more essential it is that its settlement underwrite change to our industrial relations system rather than sustain its insidious rigidities.

*****

OCTOBER 1989

Friday, 6 October 1989, p. 11

19

Howard's mantra of pursuing micro-economic reform continues. Warning that Australia's economic survival is inextricably linked to the Japanese/US economic relationship, he believes now is hardly the time to rest on our laurels. Trumpeting the old-fashioned virtues of hard work, self-reliance and thrift, Howard lists labour market, privatisation, coastal shipping and waterfront reforms as essential to lifting Australia's savings and productivity. He would pursue these reforms with vigour as prime minister.

'The continental drift to bankruptcy'

As part of our economic education the Federal Government should supply all Australian households with a free copy of 'Self-help' by Samuel Smiles.

Before saying 'self-what?' and 'Samuel who?' or imaging that I have approached some kind of metaphorical dotage, let me explain.

'Self-help' in its time was a veritable bible of British Victorian ideas on economics. It caused something of a sensation in Japan immediately after the Meiji Revolution of 1868.

The book sold a million copies to a total Japanese population then only about 30 million – a truly astonishing performance.

It extolled the virtues of collective hard work, self-reliance and thrift. Bearing in mind the fundamental role these attributes have played in the awesome economic miracle which is modern Japan my rather quirky allusion to the book is not totally facetious.

I unearthed these facts when reading Daniel Burstein's 'Yen!' which traces the recent history of the United States/Japanese economic relationship and explicitly describes how in five short years the United States went from being the world's largest creditor to the world's biggest debtor.

Reading 'Yen!' is to experience wave after wave of amazing economic statistics which illustrates the formidable financial grip of Japan.

One of those statistics illustrates the shift: the giant Merrill Lynch, known not so affectionately in Wall Street as 'the thundering herds' because of its sheer size and all-embracing activities, is now but one-twentieth of the size of Nomura Securities, the largest of the big four security houses of Tokyo.

Not all of Daniel Burstein's conclusions are ones which I share.

However, any analysis of the changed economic relationship between Japan and the United States in recent years drives home two unarguable Japanese economic virtues compellingly relevant to Australia's modern economic dilemma.

These are a high level of savings and a high level of productivity.

I have never believed that slavish comparisons can be drawn between Japan and Australia. There exist profound social and cultural divides rendering much of what occurs in Japan as irrelevant and unworkable in Australia.

Quality of life is surely never measured simply by net material assets.

However, the two areas of savings and productivity have been so integral to Japan's economic success that, like the Bourbons, we will have learnt nothing if we do not take stock of our abysmal performance in both areas.

'Savings and productivity are essential to reducing our chronic level of overseas debt'

Common consent has it that the greatest long term economic challenge is for Australia to stabilise and over time reduce her high level of foreign debt. To do this we must reduce our current account deficit by some method superior to that of crunching the life out of the economy through a severe recession.

Whilst some economists will argue about the relative importance of increasing savings as distinct from lifting productivity, most concede that enhanced performance in these two areas is essential if we are to have any hope of reducing our chronic level of overseas debt.

Independence

The Treasurer is fond of the so-called 'main game'. To me for a long time the main economic game has been tackling and reducing our foreign debt.

That task is in every sense the main game because it goes to the heart of our independence as a nation.

A nation which must continually devote an increasing share of GDP to servicing foreign debt can hardly claim true economic sovereignty.

Mr Keating may strut the world stage. His emissary, Mr Dawkins[39], may lecture the major industrial countries at the IMF regarding fiscal policy. But none of this verbal flummery alters the fact that in recent years real control of our economy has noiselessly slipped away into the hands of foreigners as our net overseas debt has soared.

As such a credible long term economic strategy to stabilise and reduce that debt must, in the name of national responsibility, dwarf any other economic policy debate as we approach the next election.

That is a view I have adhered to for a long time.

That is also why the stronger more credible commitment of the

---

39 The Honourable John Dawkins AO, Labor Minister for Trade, 13 December 1984 – 24 July 1987 later Treasurer of Australia, 27 December 1991 – 22 December 1993.

Coalition to micro economic reform, so crucial to lifting productivity, should give it a flying start on this front.

A quick look at some basic statistics show how poorly we perform in the savings and productivity areas, particularly the latter.

According to the OECD, since 1987 total factor productivity in Australia has actually fallen by 0.2 per cent against an OECD average rise of 1.2 per cent. Our performance between 1980 and 1986 was better but still below the average.

In both periods Japan and the United Kingdom performed above average with the United States being under the average in both comparisons.

The long-term savings performance of Japan compared to most industrialised countries has been well and truly documented. A popular international economic comparison a few years ago was the so-called misery index. That was a combination of unemployment and inflation. It is still in use as a relevant measure.

Given the frightening swings in national indebtedness and their importance not only to the Japanese/United States economic relationship but also Australia's economic survival, we should perhaps create another index. Let's call it the debt index. It should be a combination of productivity and savings. My rough guess would be that the poor performance on this index would be those countries such as Australia who have gone deeper and deeper into debt in recent years.

The Hawke Government likes to boast about the 1.5 million new jobs created over the last six and a half years. In itself this is a fine achievement having undoubtedly improved the living standards of those individuals and families previously without work.

Beneath the surface, however, lurks the huge productivity failure which the statistics cited above evidence. It is not scoring a cheap political point to register the fact that many of the 1.5 million new jobs have been purchased at the price of an horrendous lift in our debts to foreigners.

Failure

For much of this year the economic debate has centred around micro economic reform. We have all become thoroughly immersed in argument about the flexibility of our labour market, privatisation, coastal shipping and waterfront reforms.

Reforms in these areas are critical, not as a means of satisfying some ideological binge of market economists, but as a device to lift productivity.

Not everything about the British economy now smells of roses. Nonetheless the Thatcher years have clearly produced attitudinal shifts in British industry which have reaped enormous productivity benefits.

For the past eight years the productivity of British manufacturing has risen at 5.5 per cent per annum.

Even allowing for the appallingly low base from which this industrial resurrection commenced, it is a noteworthy achievement.

Micro economic reform, particularly in the area of labour market changes, has doubtless played a very key role in this turnaround.

One of the more pleasing things about public life in Australia over recent years has been the enormous improvement in the quality of the economic debate.

The bureaucracy's professionalism has increased. Union leadership at the ACT level has been better. Private sector economic advice has burgeoned with much being of high quality and the areas of difference between the Labor Party and the Coalition have narrowed as a result of Labor abandoning its previous feckless attitude towards budgetary restraint and its embracing of such policies as financial sector deregulation.

The very fact that the debate has narrowed to a heavy concentration on the so-called micro economic issues casts a greater onus on both sides to clearly articulate their different approaches in this area.

Unless we lift our productivity and savings game, we will not have the proverbial earthly of solving our foreign debt challenge.

Those now rather old-fashioned sounding virtues of collective hard work, self-reliance and thrift which so attracted the Japanese more than a hundred years ago are not entirely irrelevant to Australia's economic circumstances as we approach the 1990s. Indeed, they are at the very core of the problem.

*****

Friday, 13 October 1989, p. 13

20

The future of Eastern Europe is front of mind for Howard. Lessons learnt from the past are instructive as the West's victory over communist ideas begins to reshape the lives of millions of people. Urging democracies to stand shoulder to shoulder, Howard posits that consolidating victory requires an imaginative economic and political response.

'Our new comrades a capital investment'

'Now having momentarily won the battle of ideas in at least two East Bloc countries, we must do what we can to consolidate'

Winston Churchill's[40] lament that the allies having won the Great War then proceeded to lose the great peace which followed should instruct the major industrial nations of the world as they contemplate the future of Eastern Europe.

A war has been won in parts of Eastern Europe. It is far different from that of World War I. It is a victory of ideas – not of arms. It is nonetheless a notable victory. Its potential is to re-shape the political environment in which the world lives.

How permanent becomes the retreat of doctrinaire Communism in Eastern Europe is as yet unknown. The West is not a passive spectator. It has a crucial role to play.

Rather than doom ourselves to relive Churchill's lament about the lost peace of a different era and kind we of the capitalist industrialised West must do all in our power to ensure that the growing rejection of Communism in Eastern Europe is no mere aberration.

[40] The Right Honourable Sir Winston Churchill, Prime Minister of the United Kingdom, 10 May 1940 – 26 July 1945 and 26 October 1951 – 5 April 1955.

1989 has been the most momentous year for world Communism since 1917, which saw the Bolshevik revolution.

The amazing unfolding of events in Eastern Europe which has seen first Poland and, then, to a greater extent Hungary, renounce Communism and opt for an experiment in social democracy, is only part of the story.

Potentially of even greater significance has been the increased balkanisation of the Soviet Union itself.

The strains and tensions within the Soviet Union not only played a direct role in the approving response of the Soviet leadership to the changes in Poland and Hungary but also have permanent implications for the Soviet Union's long-term place in the Communist world.

The images of 1989 will all be of turmoil in the Communist world. The horror of the bloody suppression in Tiananmen Square was matched by the hundreds of thousands who joined hands across the Baltic States to commemorate the Molotov-Rippentrop Pact[41]. Then came the spectacle of East Germans chanting 'Gorby, Gorby', while thousands of their countrymen walked away from all they owned to seek refuge in the West.

To the generations whose images of Eastern Europe were Soviet tanks suppressing rebellions this has been a very heady year.

It is tempting to hope that the changes in countries such as Poland and Hungary are permanent. We should all dare to believe that having tasted the dreary collectivism of the past forty years their peoples genuinely want an alternative.

Time and experience will tell. It is simply not possible at this juncture to make any permanent judgement beyond observing the remarkable sweep of the changes which have taken place.

The more cynical may see a hidden purpose in the acquies-

---

41 The Molotov-Ribbentrop Pact was a non-aggression pact signed between Nazi Germany and the Soviet Union in Moscow on 23 August 1939.

cence of not only the Soviet leadership but also the Polish Communist Party.

Perhaps the game plan is to give the peasants a taste of democracy and the free market in the belief that early beneficial results will not be achieved (which will certainly prove to be the case) and this relative failure can pave the way for a reassertion of hard-line Communist control.

Some of the gloss of Solidarity will disappear quickly. Already Lech Walesa[42], mindful of adverse consumer reactions to price rises in Poland, has hinted of a rapid loss of popularity by the Solidarity movement. He even fears that malcontents will wreck his new home.

Rejection of Communism in Poland has a spiritual dimension as well as being a frustrated repudiation of the abject economic failures of the Communist years.

Although there were vastly differing roles and circumstances, the part played by the Catholic Church in the Polish revolution was equally as pivotal as that of the Church in bringing undone the Marcos regime in the Philippines.

The countervailing ideological force in Poland which is the Catholic Church will almost certainly prevent any voluntary return to Communist control.

'There are huge obstacles, but also huge gains'

Preoccupied with a homefront restlessly wanting a better life, the Kremlin under Gorbachev will not wish to add Soviet military clout to any hard-line Communist resurgence in Poland or, indeed, anywhere else.

This is all speculation about the future. The more pressing question is what should the West do in response to the amazing changes in Eastern Europe?

[42] President of Poland, 22 December 1990 – 22 December 1995

We must certainly do more than stand on the sidelines and applaud. The apparent crumbling of the internal cohesion of both Eastern Europe and the Soviet Union must not swamp us in self-satisfaction.

We are entitled to feel well pleased that the free market as an economic credo and personal freedom as a political ideology is having a very good year. But having momentarily won the battle of ideas in at least two East European countries we must do what we can to consolidate that victory.

Alan Greenspan[43], the Chairman of the United States Federal Reserve, is now in Moscow giving advice about restructuring the Soviet monetary system. Gestures such as this will be duplicated many times over.

However, a grander more imaginative response is needed. It is needed not only from the United States and the nations of the European community, it is also needed in full measure from Japan, ever-bursting at the seams with her current account surpluses.

Whether it is called a Marshall (Nomura!) Plan for Eastern Europe or whatever, it must be within both the wit and capacity of the G-7 nations at least to seize the great opportunity opened up by the momentous changes in Hungary and Poland.

The goal must be to help nations such as those to succeed in their bold experiment with both capitalism and political freedom. We will fail the most basic of tests of our own commitment to the values we allegedly hold dear unless this opportunity is grabbed with both hands.

I am told by one of my Parliamentary colleagues that on a recent Parliamentary delegation's visit to Hungary he was lectured by the Secretary-General of the now self-extinguished Hungarian Communist Party about the evils of collectivism and the virtues of the free market.

---

[43] 13th President of the United States Federal Reserve, 11 August 1987 – 31 January 2006.

That is the measure of the sea change which has occurred. In the name of self-interest alone we must surely try to cement the change.

It is a time for some risks and some innovation. It is also an occasion for American leadership.

Her economic dominance may be diminished but her political and diplomatic clout, even in Eastern Europe, and most certainly in encouraging the interest of Japan, is unmatched.

The potential for all forms of foreign investment in Eastern Europe is considerable – particularly from the Japanese.

There is no reason why some of the huge savings of Japanese now acquiring real estate in California and the Gold Coast cannot buy villas on the Danube. More pertinently, Japanese high tech and capital investment coupled with the highly competitive labour rates of Eastern Europe could finally spark life into the lagging manufacturing industries of the Eastern bloc.

The European Commission already shares a joint Commission with the Comintern (Eastern bloc) countries. Why not start negotiations with Poland or Hungary or both for some kind of associate membership of the European Commission?

There are huge obstacles but also huge gains to be had. This is something of a moment in history where even the demonstration effect of a bold initiative will have a powerful impact.

Some Australian companies such as BHP, Elders and TNT, have already blazed a trail in Eastern Europe. They and others like them should be given every reasonable encouragement – yet another reason for the Government to abandon its foolish foreign tax credit system which discourages Australian companies from investing abroad.

Moreover, the psychological effect of massive Western financial involvement in Poland or Hungary on countries such as East Germany and Romania which remain hard line would be enormous.

It might be one of the pressures which dissuades Eric Honecker[44] from invoking the Beijing option.

The peaceful transfer of power and renunciation of ideology in part of Eastern Europe has few, if any, parallels since World War II. We can hope it is genuine, permanent and the harbinger of like change in other parts of the Eastern bloc.

It may not be, and we should reserve all the appropriate levels of cynicism.

However, the helping hand of the capitalist West could well tilt the scales. That is why we should act and act boldly.

*****

[44] General Secretary of the Socialist Unity Party of Germany, 3 May 1971 – 18 October 1989.

Friday, 20 October 1989, p. 13

21

'It's the economy, stupid', is the essence of Howard's message. Two years on from Paul Keating's famous 'banana republic' statement, Howard is concerned for Australia's low productivity levels, rising inflation, and increasing overseas debt. Placing his faith in markets to provide best economic outcomes, Howard's tenacious view of favouring a private sector-led recovery and a limiting role for government remains unwavering.

'Living on the economic fault line'

It is an eerie coincidence that the San Francisco earthquake and a tremor of a different kind on Wall Street should have occurred within a few days of each other.

Of the many images there are of the United States this century the great San Francisco earthquake of 1906 and the Wall Street crash of 1929 are amongst the more powerful.

To the generations of Australians raised on Hollywood movies of the 1940s and 1950s in particular, these two events frequently featured.

The parallels do not end there. Despite a nerve-wracking weekend, Wall Street last Monday did not produce a repeat performance of the Monday after the Friday of 1987.

It almost seems as though the latest threat to the stability of world stock markets has come and gone in 72 hours. By the same token and despite all the doomsday talk, the 1987 collapse did not bring about economic ruin of the kind that followed the 1929 crash.

In relative terms the aftershock from last Friday's fall on the New York stock exchange will almost certainly be far more benign that that which followed the 1987 dive.

All of this means that the world has got better at containing potential financial disaster. By common consent the central banks of the major industrial countries displayed masterly management following October 1987.

Unlike their 1929 financial forebears they did not crunch the life out of the monetary system thereby dooming many large financial institutions to a certain death.

That had been all the more culpable given that the 1929 collapse followed a time during which the world's banking system had been positively profligate in allowing the enormous accumulation of debt.

Grim though yesterday's news from San Francisco is, it is almost certainly the case that the tragic experience of 1906 taught many lessons which have reduced the loss of life and damage more than 80 years later.

On both earthquake fronts – financial and seismological – experience has been a useful teacher. That is the good news.

The bad news is, of course, the awful loss of life in San Francisco coupled with the ominous realisation that the 'big one' in the form of another really major earthquake could occur on the San Andreas fault line within the next few decades.

On the financial front, the really bad news for Australia from the stock market gyrations of the last week is that once again we have been brutally and instantaneously reminded that, come Hell or high water, we are totally and utterly part of the world financial system.

Instantaneous communications and the 24-hour world market have produced something akin to a perpetual world test match.

Last Monday when I listened to the early morning news that

the Barclays Index in New Zealand had fallen 10 per cent in the first hour I had a strange feeling. The newsreader could almost have been saying that after an hour's play England were 3 for 25. But then, of course, that would be good news!

Give or take some relative minor variations, Australian stock markets almost faithfully followed Wall Street. Significantly, our exchanges appeared to fall further on Monday than many experts had deemed necessary given the size of the Wall Street fall the previous Friday.

The collective view quickly emerged that once Wall Street had recovered when it re-opened on Monday any major crisis was unlikely to emerge.

This irreversible identification with the rest of the financial world underlines the extraordinary vulnerability of the Australian economy. It reminds us yet again of how nationally culpable we are to have accumulated such a huge level of debt to the world banking system.

On Page 8 of the Economic Action Plan released by the Coalition parties last week is the table that is the most compelling part of the document.

Compiled from BIS Shrapnel and the OECD, the table disclosed that Australia was now third in a list of countries ranked according to the level of external debt they owe to commercial banks.

I am sure it would astonish most Australians to know that according to the table the only countries with a higher external debt exposure are Brazil and Mexico and that our exposure is even worse than that of both the Soviet Union and Argentina.

In 1986, just after Mr Keating had warned of banana republican status, the Government adopted the solemn line that our balance of trade and hence gathering overseas debt problem was all the fault of foreigners.

Those wicked people had stopped paying us decent prices for

our commodities. They had wiped $9 billion off our national income, declared the Prime Minister. If only we could reverse that then all would be well.

Ironically enough in subsequent years we did in fact reverse much of that. Our terms of trade recovered dramatically, and the Treasurer stopped whining in Parliament about the poor returns our producers were receiving for certain commodities.

'Only Mexico and Brazil have a worse debt exposure than us'

While in recent months there have been some signs of a weakening in commodity prices, the past year has still been strong. In the absence of a dramatic fall-off in world economic growth our commodity prices as a whole are unlikely to go into free fall.

If, however, the world rate of economic growth did pull up sharply, that would inevitably depress commodity prices and an already huge overseas debt problem would be further exacerbated.

However, our fundamental debt problem is not and never has been the fault of foreigners. It is essentially home grown. It is a product of too much consumption given a stagnant level of production, compounded by a grievous absence of domestic savings which compels us to draw on the savings of foreigners.

We can hardly blame the foreigners for having the cash to bail us out of our home grown predicament.

The English poet, Housman, once wrote of 'the idle hill of summer'. It seems a particularly apt and evocative phrase to describe the state of mind of many in the Australian community regarding our overseas debt problem.

There is an idle indifference to it; plenty of ritualistic acknowledgement that the problem exists yet concrete decisions go completely in the wrong direction.

The worst example in recent times was, of course, Coronation Hill. It passes all comprehension that a nation facing the trade and debt crisis of the magnitude which now confronts Australia could possibly countenance such a recklessly cynical and economically irresponsible decision.

It would not have escaped the attention of many that the Tokyo stock exchange showed it had a life all its own in the wake of the Wall Street fall. Nor would it entirely surprise if in the days ahead stories emerge of strategic institutional and government decisions having been taken in Japan which bore heavily upon the failure of the United Airlines buy-out which a lot of market analysts claim to be the immediate trigger for last Friday's 190-point dive in the Dow.

The apologists for re-regulation will probably claim that the stability of the Nikkei Index results from there being a lot more de facto regulation and government control in Japan.

It is true that the big institutions work cheek by jowl, with the Ministry of Finance. However, as the saying goes, one must have strings to the bow. All the concerted government private sector action in the world won't amount to much if the economic fundamentals are wrong.

When it comes to the debt problem, Japan's economic fundamentals are overwhelmingly right. She has huge current account surpluses, is the world's largest creditor, has high levels of productivity and a high savings ratio.

It will not last forever. As Gregory Clark pointed out on these pages last week, Japan will in future years feel the full effect of the sharp contraction in her birthrate after World War II.

In Australia, those same economic fundamentals are overwhelmingly wrong.

We run a huge current account deficit, are in hock to the rest of the world, have experienced productivity levels below the OECD average, and have a pathetic savings ratio. Add to this an inflation rate now nearly double the OECD average and a fairly sorry picture emerges.

Those who basically place their faith in markets to provide the best economic outcomes – and I am one – hold rather tenaciously to the view that the role of government should be limited to providing incentives to influence economic behaviour. It should never be to guarantee market shares for particular economic players. Nor should it seek to impose government commercial decisions upon private sector participants.

So much of what is now economically wrong in Australia is the product of past government attempts to do exactly this: our incentives structure is all wrong: there are inadequate incentives to save and far too many incentives to consume; and within our labour markets incentives for enterprise-level collaboration are virtually non-existent.

In the United States it is fashionable to talk about the twin deficit evil. In Australia it is the twin evil of low savings and low productivity. They have spawned our huge overseas debt. The past week has warned us yet again that all our policy energies as a nation must be directed to lifting savings and productivity.

*****

Friday, 27 October 1989, p. 11

22

Queensland, beautiful one day ... political the next. Howard's topsy-turvy relationship continues unabated with the Queensland Nationals. Insisting the Russell Cooper-led government has done little to reform itself ahead of the state election, Howard's lament is writ large. He predicts an end to conservative rule in Queensland. Labor's Wayne Goss would go on to secure victory on 2 December. (Notably, Howard would go on to win 23 of 26 Queensland seats at the 1996 Federal election, with a swing of 8.3 per cent to the Liberal/ National coalition.)

'Nats disqualify themselves from serious poll contention'

To vary the well-known TV advertisement, one could well say: Queensland politics – fascinating one day, unbelievable the next.

Queensland is different, and in some respects different in the nicest possible way.

Over the past year millions of words have been written analysing the different traits of Queensland politics and attempting to discover the forces at work within Queensland society.

Some of this analysis has been pushed too far to discover explanations.

Such differences as do exist between Queensland politics and those of other Australian States are due more than anything else to one rather obvious fact. Unlike the rest of the Australian mainland, Queensland is the only State in which the majority of the population lives outside the capital city. This fact has had more bearing on the course of Queensland politics than anything else.

It has not been the only difference at work, but it has clearly been the most dominant.

The forthcoming Queensland election will be filled with interest for the politically addicted, and I suspect many more.

It presents the honest, sincere conservative voter who believes in the true working of the democratic process with something of a dilemma.

It is beyond doubt that the Queensland National Party has badly let down the conservative cause in recent years.

The disastrous 'Joh for PM' campaign which did more than anything else to re-elect the Hawke Government in 1987, together with the administrative and other failures revealed by the Fitzgerald Report, should on any normal criteria disqualify the Queensland Nationals from any voice in the next Government of Queensland.

Their failure on these two fronts was compounded by the wilful and wholly unnecessary dumping of the former Premier, Michael Ahern[45], at the behest of the Queensland National Party organisation.

Mr Ahern may have had his weaknesses. He may have backed and filled over daylight saving for example – although his ultimate decision was the right one.

However, on the central issue of the day, namely the endemic corruption disclosed by the Fitzgerald Report, Michael Ahern was headed in the right direction.

He had a clear view that a new era of open, accountable government was needed in Queensland.

I remember a conversation with him shortly after he became Premier of Queensland when he said to me, 'It's got to be cleaned up. We have got to do this for our kids.'

They struck me as the words of a man who recognised some past failings by his own Party and who was resolved to put things right no matter what the personal cost.

---

[45] The Honourable Mike Ahern AO, 32nd Premier of Queensland, 1 December 1987 – 25 September 1989.

In political terms the personal cost to him was very high indeed. The ultimate judgement of political history will almost certainly be a lot kinder to him than were his Parliamentary colleagues.

It is difficult to escape the conclusion that Ahern was sand-bagged because he was travelling too fast down the Fitzgerald path of reform.

His successor dragged his feet on the Fitzgerald reforms until Fitzgerald himself cut loose at the North Melbourne VFL breakfast a few weeks ago. After this the new Queensland Premier changed his tack.

In a sense, however, it was too late. The perception remains that Ahern's zeal for reform and desire to clean up the State of Queensland was a little too close for comfort.

Now that the campaign has started Russell Cooper's[46] refrain is that all conservative supporters in Queensland, whether National or Liberal, should stand shoulder to shoulder against the Labor flood.

That would be an admirable exhortation if it reeked of consistency and did not proclaim the expediency of a man who knows in his heart that the Queensland Nationals have no hope of winning a majority in their own right.

'Vote Liberal and hope – like hell'

Such appeals to conservative unity turns on its head almost ten years of Queensland National Party rhetoric which more often than not bracketed the Liberal Party with the worst excesses of the Left Wing of the Labor Party.

The Queensland Labor leader, Wayne Goss[47], is articulate and superficially popular but he leads an unimpressive, lacklustre Par-

---

[46] The Honourable Russell Cooper AO, 33rd Premier of Queensland, 25 September 1989 – 7 December 1989, a period of 73 days.

[47] The Honourable Wayne Goss, 34th Premier of Queensland, 7 December 1989 – 19 February 1996.

liamentary team which as recently as three months ago did not have the elementary Parliamentary discipline to secure the attendance of all its members during a vital division over the Speakership of the House.

Such laxity would never have been permitted by Neville Wran[48] or Brian Burke[49] as Opposition Leaders on the verge of assuming power.

It is also an undeniable fact that, notwithstanding some of the excesses, Queensland has been a good State in which to do business. There is nothing inherently wrong with a collective government will to cut bureaucratic red tape and speed up government approval for business transactions. It only becomes malicious and corrupt when favours are done and money changes hand.

The third man in Queensland politics is Angus Innes[50]. He is honest, intelligent and has grown in stature in his position.

The Liberal leader in Queensland has had a difficult path to tread. On the one hand he has had to differentiate his Party's product from the National Party in the eyes of conservative voters.

Yet he has had to do it in a manner that has not appeared to be an automatic endorsement of the Labor Opposition's criticism of the incumbent Government.

Mr Innes has essentially struck the right balance.

This time around the Queensland Nationals will not be saying that a vote for the Liberals is a vote for chaos. This rhetoric helped Bjelke-Petersen[51] swing the 1986 election his way during the last week. It must also be assumed that this time around Sir

---

48 The Honourable Neville Wran AC, QC, 35th Premier of New South Wales, 14 May 1976 – 4 July 1986.

49 The Honourable Brian Burke, 23rd Premier of Western Australia, 25 February 1983 – 25 February 1988.

50 Leader of the Queensland Liberal Party, 31 January 1988 – 13 May 1990.

51 The Honourable Sir Joe Bjelke-Petersen KCMG, 31st Premier of Queensland, 8 August 1968 – 1 December 1987.

Robert Sparkes'[52] treasure chest will not be as large as on earlier occasions.

If I am any judge the Nationals will spend the final week of the campaign begging Queenslanders to vote either National or Liberal as long as it is not Labor.

The Nationals warrant a spell on the sidelines. Their organisation deserves a clean out. If accountability in government has any meaning they have failed some of the most basic tests, particularly in view of the removal of Ahern.

If he had remained then at least he could have sought a mandate on the basis that he was making things different.

Given the zonal system it is almost beyond hope that the Liberal Party can win in its own right. Liberal seniority between the two conservative parties is possible and the Liberals have made this a condition of any future coalition Government.

There are those who condemn the Liberal Party's stance on coalition as hypocritical.

This charge can be made but on close examination it is surely unreasonable.

Short of conceding the election to Labor, which is unthinkable, the Queensland Liberals have no realistic alternative.

They are right to reject the junior role in any coalition with the Nationals.

In fact, if they were to indicate a willingness to play second fiddle this would probably increase the Labor vote.

Such acquiescence could easily be painted by Labor as offering a re-run of the past.

Not only would that alienate many swinging voters but also those conservative voters who don't want a Labor Government but, with almost equal fervour, do not wish the National Party to effectively run the next Queensland Government.

---

52 President of the Queensland National Party, 1970 – 1990.

The Liberals are saying that a Liberal-led conservative coalition government offers the best of both worlds. It is an alternative to Labor without the National Party excesses of the past.

My advice to the conscientious conservative voter of Queensland troubled by events of recent years but not wanting a Labor Government is to vote Liberal and hope like hell they win enough seats to be the major party in a coalition government.

*****

NOVEMBER 1989

Friday, 3 November 1989, p. 11

23

In his final article, Howard reflects on a decade of dramatic change: capitalism and free enterprise trumping collectivism in Eastern Europe at an astonishing pace (the Berlin Wall was to fall a week later), the rise of Japan as an economic powerhouse, price stability driving global economic growth, and a narrowing of economic differences between Australia's two major parties. Concerned for an ever-increasing level of overseas debt, Howard remains optimistic for the new decade.

'Braving the '90s on a surge of optimism'

No decade in my lifetime has ended on a more optimistic note than the 1980s. Politically there is more cause for genuine hope amongst the nations of the world than probably at any time since the end of World War II.

The projected summit between President Bush and President Gorbachev is but the latest example of the still tentative but growing trust between the United States and the Soviet Union.

Economically the message from the '80s has been the extraordinary victory throughout the world of capitalism and free enterprise over collectivism. Not only have the free market parties within the democratic world held the ascendancy, but the nominally social democratic parties have shifted a long way to the right.

Most spectacularly of all, countries in Eastern Europe such as Hungary have forcefully repudiated their old economic ways.

In economic terms the 1970s will best be remembered for the huge economic realignments caused by the successive oil shocks of 1974 and 1979.

These produced high inflation and balance of payments crises for many countries.

No industrialised nation was more severely affected by the two oil shocks than Japan whose total reliance on imported oil necessitated a gigantic economic adjustment.

It is therefore both ironic and salutary to the rest of the industrialised world that one of the features of the 1980s has been Japan's continued rise to a position of such economic strength. Amongst other things she is the largest creditor nation in the world.

There was much in the 1980s which gave cause for optimism.

We are now in the eighth year of the longest period of economic growth the major industrialised nations have experienced since World War II. Much of the key to this has been the infinitely greater price stability which almost all of those countries have experienced in recent years.

If one were obliged to nominate an economic hero of the 1980s it would unquestionably be Paul Volker.[53]

When he went to the Federal Reserve in the late 1970s inflation in the United States was running out of control at approximately 17 per cent. His resolute prosecution of monetary discipline, his refusal to bend to many of the snake oil answers around at the time, more than anything else dragged down the US inflation rate and for the first time since the mid-1960s induced an obsession with keeping prices down in the United States which went close to matching that in both Japan and West Germany.

The greatest success story of the 1980s was the skilful handling by the world central banks of the aftermath of the 1987 stock market crash.

To those who perpetually peddle gloom on economic matters this was an object lesson. Unlike 1929 the central banks avoided a counter-productive response.

---

[53] Paul Volker was the 12th Chairman of the United States Federal Reserve, 6 August 1979 – 11 August 1987.

Here in Australia the 1980s have been characterised more than anything by an astronomical rise in our overseas debt levels. That is not to say there have not been gains made on the economic front.

Importantly, for those who care about long term solutions, the quality of economic debate in Australia has lifted dramatically over the last five to ten years.

To start with, there is a far greater appreciation now than ever before of the impact of world economic events on Australia.

The floating of the exchange rate in 1983 for all time ended any real notions within Australia that in some way Australia could indulge some cosseted existence free from the buffeting of global economic pressures.

That is not to say that there are not many in Australia who still believe that we can retreat to insularity and that our current economic problems are the product of financial deregulation and that if only we returned to the days of controls some of the pain could be reduced.

The fact is that Australia has always been vulnerable to overseas economic forces. The great change wrought by the floating of the dollar was that from then on the economic signals from abroad were transmitted directly and instantaneously. They could no longer be muffled by government intervention.

'It is possible the world may have changed for the better'

Of course, not all of the government intervention in exchange rate management before 1983 was wrong. Indeed, one of the more absurd myths peddled by the Treasurer is that the floating of the dollar in December 1983 dramatically ended an artificially high exchange rate.

The fatal flaw in this proposition is that after the float there was no dramatic change in the value of the Australian dollar freely traded for over twelve months. It was not until early in 1985 when cumulative doubts arose within financial markets about the Hawke Government's resolve, particularly in the wake of the MX missile fiasco, that the big slide in the A$ began.

Nonetheless a floating exchange rate is vastly superior to a managed system, not least because it cannot conceal the truth about the attitude of other nations and financial markets towards the conduct of domestic economic policy.

The discipline imposed by the floating of the dollar has played a major part in changing the nature and improving the quality of the economic debate in Australia.

It has played a role in bringing about some of the important attitudinal shifts amongst key groups in the Australian community. For example, the present leadership of the trade union movement displays a vastly superior understanding of the nature of the Australian economy and its difficulties than did their predecessors in the late 1970s.

The parameters of the economic debate between the major parties has narrowed, especially in the area of budget policy. Differences remain there but they are of degree rather than amounting to sharply varying approaches.

The economic battleground of the 1990s will unquestionably be not only the areas which must be subject to major economic reform, but the pace at which that reform occurs.

The 1980s was the era of financial market deregulation. The 1990s must be the era of labour market deregulation.

One of the great ironies is that the sheer magnitude of the change brought about by freeing the exchange rate made it all the more necessary to take matching domestic action in areas such as the labour market.

The rhetoric of both the Labor Party and the trade unions has undergone a significant change on this subject. They no longer decry the need for labour market reform. However, they now argue that such reform can best be achieved from within the existing system. Award restructuring has become to the Government the essence of industrial relations change.

The grave weakness in this argument and where the Government's approach is sharply deficient to that of the Opposition is that unless there are fundamental changes to the system itself via removal of the monopoly powers of trade unions there can be no lasting reform.

Change in this area lies at the heart of reform in areas such as coastal shipping, the waterfront, communications and transport. So much of the tardiness of the Government in these areas is a direct consequence of it being unwilling to confront monopoly union power with the necessary reforms.

The wimpish Willis waterfront package is a case in point.

However, I have been talking here of mechanisms rather than goals.

Successfully persuading a hesitant and doubting public about the need for change can only be realised if expressed in terms of goals.

Labour market reform is not an end in itself. I have no quarrel with the important role of trade unions in our community. I simply see their monopoly powers in certain areas as an impediment to lifting the productivity of this country.

Australia's huge overseas debt will not be stabilised, let alone reduced, without a dramatic lift in our productivity. This in turn can only be achieved if, through aggressive labour market and other reforms, we sweep away the restrictive practices, the featherbedding, the easy life attitude of many areas of management, which are a severe impediment.

This is why our greatest economic goal of the 1990s must be to lift our national productivity.

Taking a world view, there is a lot to be optimistic about. Relations between the superpowers are better. The liberalisation process in Eastern Europe has moved at a truly astonishing pace. The voluntary retreat of authoritarian Communism has surpassed the dreams of the most optimistic even a few years ago. Without forsaking caution, it is possible to believe that the world may indeed have changed for the better.

We must bring this same sense of optimism to our own domestic problems. The political and social cohesion Australia enjoys, together with our vast natural resources, give us a start in tackling problems which few countries have. This makes it all the more necessary that we adequately match the challenge to turn around our national productivity.

*****

As I have returned to the Opposition frontbench this is my valedictory column for 'The Australian'. I thank 'The Australian' and, in particular its editor Frank Devine, for the opportunity to write over recent months which I have found immensely satisfying.

Afterword

John Howard

Shortly after I was removed as Liberal Party Leader in May 1989, Paul Kelly, now editor-at-large at the Australian Newspaper, asked me if I would write a regular column for the paper, whose then editor-in-chief was Frank Devine. I jumped at the offer.

So began a very pleasurable experience of penning a regular column for the national newspaper. I enjoyed the experience immensely and found writing on any manner of subjects anything but a chore.

The late Frank Devine, a larger-than-life editor, who was possessed of a great sense of humour, offered occasional pieces of counsel in the first weeks of my new assignment. The most valuable advice he gave was that I should always strive to simplify what I was saying. I always tried hard to follow that advice.

Naturally most of my columns were about politics. Yet there was the odd excursion into sport such as an early one paying tribute to Alan Border's leadership of the Australian Cricket team when the Ashes were reclaimed in 1989.

Although I was no longer a member of the Coalition front bench and had the freedom to write as I chose, I remained committed to the return of a Liberal/National Party government. Nonetheless on occasions, such as during the pilots' strike, I argued for an outcome consistent with the long-held views I had expressed on industrial relations. The official Coalition position was a little different. I also expressed strong opinions on Queensland politics, conditioned by my bruising experience during the chaotic 'Joh for PM' years.

I enjoyed being something of a part-time journalist, recalling that in my final year at Canterbury Boys High School in 1956,

I had nominated journalism as one of the three occupations I would consider pursuing. Incidentally, the three I nominated did not include politics. That was a time when politics was regarded as something one pursued after a primary career in some other field. In more recent years more and more people enter parliament having done nothing other than work in politics before becoming a Member of Parliament. As is well known I believe this development has its drawbacks.

I am delighted that this collection of my journalistic offerings has been put together. Naturally I have re-read all the pieces I composed more than 30 years ago. There is not much I would like to take back. That is a source of some satisfaction because what I wrote more than three decades ago was consistent with the *broad-church* Liberalism I have long espoused.

Values such as individual freedom, private enterprise, pride in one's country and respect for the role of the family are timeless. They are as relevant today for the Liberal Party and Australia as they were more than 30 years ago.

Appendices

Appendix 1

THE AUSTRALIAN

2 Holt St., Surry Hills, Sydney, Australia. Tel: (02) 288 3000. G.P.O. Box 4245, N.S.W. 2002. Telex: 20124

19th May 1989

The Hon. John Howard, M.P.,
Parliament House,
Canberra
ACT 2600

Dear John,

To confirm our arrangements of yesterday. The Australian will pay you $800 a shot for a weekly column of about 1200 words, largely on national affairs, beginning Friday, June 2. For the first month at least I will be your editor and will clear with you any changes I propose. Copy should be delivered by Thursday morning to our Melbourne office, fax number 03 652 2803, although we will take it later (or make changes up to 6.00pm Thursday) if events or a major author change of mind overtake us.

This is a pretty exciting undertaking, I think. Winston Churchill and Jack Kennedy (and Eleanor Roosevelt!) come to mind especially as persons of affairs who were genuinely distinguished as journalists.

My main advice to you as one journalist to another consists of four points: (1) Decide on a single subject/theme for each column and don't be tempted to embrace other subjects that may be on your mind; (2) Fill each column with factual information and miss no opportunity to toss in a good anecdote; (3) Be John Howard; quirks and enthusiasms are very much the stuff of serious popular journalism, alien as they may be to ministerial statements; (4) No columnist should try to emulate another but the best political columnist in the world is Bill Safire of the New York Times.

Avanti!

FRANK DEVINE
Editor

RECEIVED
26 MAY 1989
Referred to:
Subject:
By:

32+41

bourne (03) 652 2888 • Canberra (062) 48 5888 • Brisbane (07) 253 3308 • Adelaide (08) 51 0351 • Perth (09) 328 1565 • Hobart (002) 34

A signed letter from Frank Devine, Editor, *The Australian*, confirming arrangements with John Howard to pay him '$800 a shot for a weekly column', beginning Friday, 2 June 1989.

Appendix 2

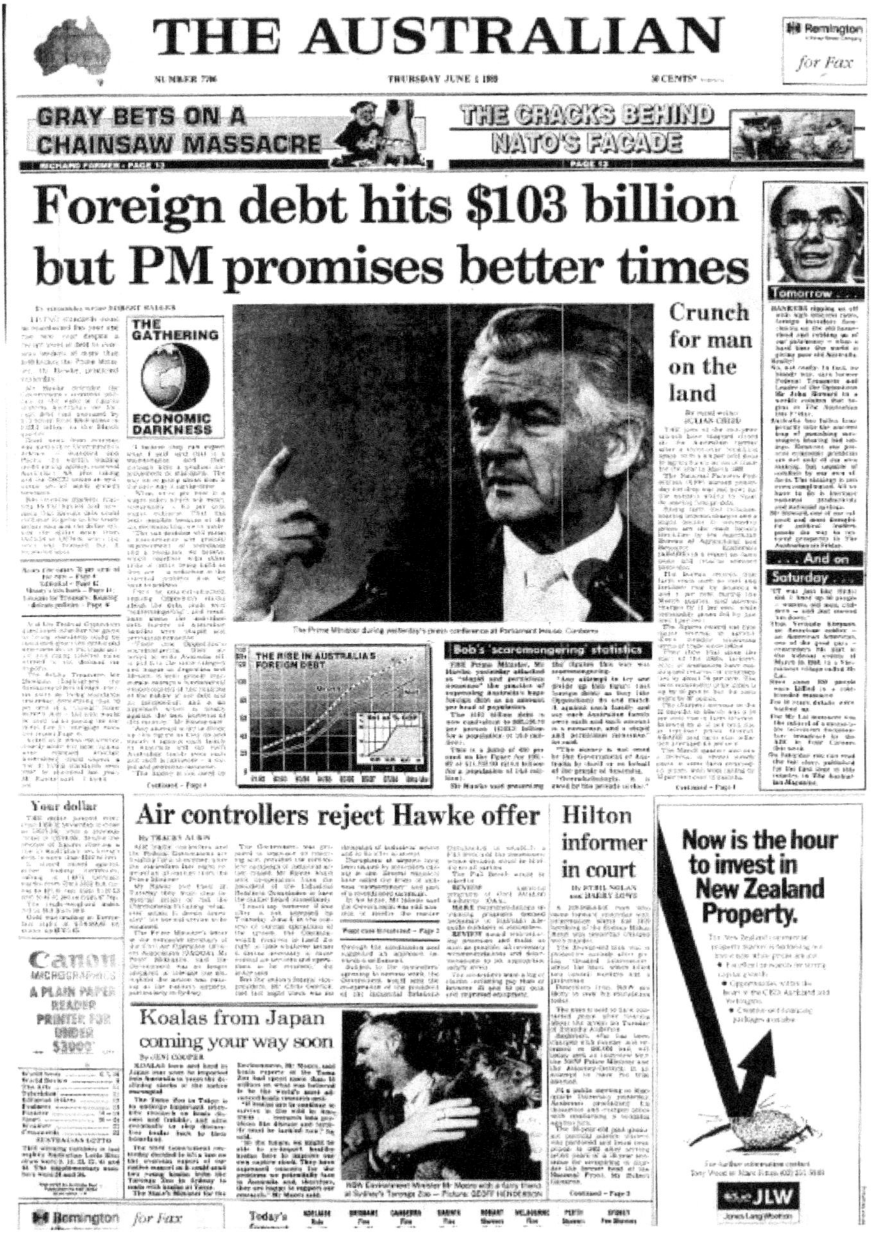

THE AUSTRALIAN

THURSDAY JUNE 1 1989

GRAY BETS ON A CHAINSAW MASSACRE

THE CRACKS BEHIND NATO'S FACADE

Foreign debt hits $103 billion but PM promises better times

THE GATHERING ECONOMIC DARKNESS

Crunch for man on the land

Tomorrow ...

... And on Saturday ...

The Prime Minister during yesterday's press conference at Parliament House, Canberra

THE RISE IN AUSTRALIA'S FOREIGN DEBT

Bob's 'scaremongering' statistics

Your dollar

Air controllers reject Hawke offer

Hilton informer in court

Canon MICROGRAPHICS A PLAIN PAPER READER PRINTER FOR UNDER $3000

Koalas from Japan coming your way soon

NSW Environment Minister Mr Moore with a furry friend at Sydney's Taronga Zoo

Now is the hour to invest in New Zealand Property.

JLW

Remington for Fax

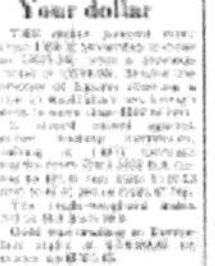

Front page, *The Australian*, Thursday, 1 June 1989, with an editorial previewing John Howard's column and regarding him as 'one of our calmest and most thoughtful political leaders'.

Appendix 3

THE AUSTRALIAN

NUMBER 7707 FRIDAY JUNE 2 1989 50 CENTS*

Remington *for Fax*

MY LAI: FINALLY, THE TRUTH TOMORROW

Waterfront under notice

But 'sharpen up' order is rapped as too soft

By LAURA TINGLE

"It is the Government which must force the pace of change in attitudes of people who play a significant role in the structure of the economy. Yesterday's statement shows just how much of a leadership vacuum has built up in Canberra in recent months."

Laura Tingle comments – Page 4

Mr Payne at Sydney Harbour yesterday ... 'We challenge any other industry to match the improvements in shipping' – Picture: COLIN MURTY

Shipowners reject golden handshakes

By JOHN SPIERS

AIDS virus 'hides in body' for three years

Continued – Page 2

Your dollar

Joh admits pushing for promotion of 'supportive judge'

By SYBIL NOLAN

Sir Joh at the judges inquiry yesterday

More to pay child support

Lean pickings on Libs' policy bone

Front page, *The Australian*, Friday, 2 June 1989.

Appendix 4

Religion

True prophets pay real dividends . . .

JAMES S. MURRAY

‘Society needs honest voices’

A disturbing case of messenger's disease

JOHN HOWARD

‘Joining a lynch-mob chorus against foreign investors won't lower interest rates’

Analysis

Why doctors feel poorly

By ROBIN BROMBY

‘Most GPs believe they have lost patients' trust’

Howard's inaugural column, *The Australian*, Friday, 2 June 1989, p. 13

Appendix 5

‘He has brought considerable credit to Australia . . . he has won, and won well’

Comment

A sportsman bordering on true greatness

JOHN HOWARD

…KNOW it is sacrilegious, in …sporting sense, to com-…nce a tribute to Allan Bor-…r with a reference to one of …e great American baseball …yers.

…at when Allan Border led …s team to cricket fame two …eks ago, I was put in mind …that Simon and Garfunkel …of the late 1960s: ‘Where have you gone Joe …Maggio? Our nation turns …lonely eyes to you.’

…n a way, the search for a …aightforward sporting …ro about which Simon and …rfunkel intoned seemed to …very apt for Allan Border.

…his column is in praise of …an Border. Not for the …st obvious reason that he …the Australians in regain… the Ashes on English soil …the first time in 56 years. …because he has become …of the truly prolific run-…ers in Australia's Test …ket history.

…hese are, in themselves, …rthy reasons for the many …olades heaped on his …ulders over the past two …eks.

…bove that, Allan Border …erves our praise and grat-…de because he is an out-…nding reminder of what …stralian sportsmanship …always supposed to be …ut.

…espite the latter-day lion-…tion of the ‘knock ’em …m, smash their teeth, …rder ’em’ philosophy of …stralian sport, which is not …y viewed from time to …e on television but prac-…d regularly by some par-…s on the sidelines of Sat-…ay morning football, Bor-… has reminded all of us …t true sportsmanship is a …bination of winning and …ce.

…e has reminded us that we …be proud of our sporting …oes, even if they do not al-…s win one for Australia.

…order has gone through …rough times, tasted de-…, faced up to the pressure …displayed great resil-…e. At the end of this he …won and won well. And, …ourse, winning well is as …ortant as losing well.

…order's magnanimous re-…ks about David Gower, …England captain, and his …inctive modesty in recal-… the valleys of despair …ough which he passed on …long march to his trea-…d moment of triumph at …Trafford, are the hall-…ks of a true sportsman.

…ey also mark him as a …who not only under-…ds the supreme impera-… of winning in competi-… sport, but also the …ally high calling of pre-…ing the better values of …ket, which is a game so …libly a part of our na-…al psyche.

…e tell our children of the …d for dogged persever-…: all the old cliches about …ng again if at first you …t succeed come to mind. …have a living example of …in Allan Border is a real …ntal bonus. It would have been easy for him to have lapsed into oafish gloating. After all, he had seen off in his time several England captains and mastered all their bowlers.

And he had received a fearful bucketing from the now discredited Fleet Street sportswriters when he and his men arrived in Britain. (Many were foolish enough to call the team the worst side Australia had sent to England since World War II.)

Through his difficult years as captain, Border has suffered many indignities, including a gratuitous piece of abuse from the present Prime Minister who, when the team was doing poorly, called it a ‘national disgrace’.

When I read of Border's generous comments regarding Gower, I was reminded of a recent statement by Sir Donald Bradman, who said: ‘When considering the stature of an athlete, or for that matter any person, I set great store on certain qualities which I believe to be essential in addition to skill.

‘Combination of courage and modesty’

‘They are that the person conducts his or her life with dignity, with integrity, with courage and perhaps most of all with modesty. These virtues are totally compatible with pride, ambition and competitiveness.’

I can think of few Australian sportsmen in recent years who fit that description more accurately than Allan Border.

He has combined skill, success and monumental achievement with the maintenance of courage, tenacity and modesty. To these he has added magnanimity in victory.

All of this has been carried out in an unpretentious and direct manner. In many interviews given during his long career, Border has never been anything other than authentic and convincing.

When he has been in the doldrums, that has shown. And when he spoke his sympathy for Gower, he clearly meant it.

Border assumed the captaincy unexpectedly from Kim Hughes in 1984. Through some incredibly bad patches and in the face of enormous criticism and ridicule, he has emerged not only triumphant as a captain but has maintained an exceptional performance as a batsman.

His greatest success over those years has been the response he has evoked from his own players. His determination and commitment has heartened them.

The partnership he has forged with team manager Bob Simpson has played a significant part in our cricket revival.

As I reflect on the achievements of Border and Simpson, I recall a Cabinet discussion during the Fraser government. We had decided to spend more money on sport and the debate was all about where it would be spent.

The general push was to put almost all of the extra funds into areas that would train and help the high achievers.

A few ministers queried this, and one former colleague retorted that sport in Australia was all about winning.

In one sense he was right. At the time there was widespread concern that, as a nation, we were not sufficiently supporting our best athletes. The initiatives born from that discussion have been of lasting benefit to Australian sport.

In a broader sense, sport is not only about winning. The drugs-in-sport drama is an example of the win-at-any-cost mentality carried to its logical conclusion. Few sporting episodes are more likely to induce cynicism among the young.

How good it is, then, to have in Allan Border someone who has not sought to win at any cost, but made it anyway and brought great credit to Australia.

As a batsman, Border is a model of patient application, great consistency and all-round ability. There is a lot of the quiet hero about him.

We haven't had many of them lately. We've had plenty of the noisy variety, whose star soars for a while and then crashes down. In the age of television, the noisy ones perhaps grab our attention more readily.

But it is still the quiet, consistent achievers such as Border, who do more to build national pride.

His success challenges some of the prevailing cynicism of our time. So much about Australia these days invokes cynicism. We need heroes and we need, from time to time, to beat cynicism, or we will not have much of a future.

One way of doing this is simply to let the spotlight pause for a while on those sportsmen and women who display grace under pressure and then go on to win with grace.

Allan Border is such a person.

Howard celebrating Allan Border’s triumph of reclaiming The Ashes, *The Australian*, 11 August 1989, p. 13

Appendix 6

11 – THE AUSTRALIAN Friday November 3 1989 – 11

South Africa

One against the rest, boldly marching in line with reform

The British Prime Minister, Margaret Thatcher, despite angry clashes with the Australian Prime Minister, Bob Hawke, was quite happy to be one against 48 in her stand at the Commonwealth Heads of Government Meeting over sanctions and South Africa. Here she explains her stance

‘It is repugnant that those people decide who will suffer poverty and starvation’

‘There will be one country it can thank for its economy: Britain’

Comment

Braving the ’90s on a surge of optimism

JOHN HOWARD

‘It is possible the world may have changed for the better’

Our Word

How not to be too personal

By BUZZ KENNEDY

Europe

The cracks in the Community

By MARK CHIPPERFIELD

‘European nations still divided on a number of logistical problems’

Howard’s valedictory column, *The Australian*, Friday, 3 November 1989, p. 11, sharing the page with his political ally, UK Prime Minister Margaret Thatcher, and an editorial comment noting John Howard ending his time as a columnist as he ‘has secured other employment’ – notably returning to the shadow Cabinet.

www.ingramcontent.com/pod-product-compliance
Lightning Source LLC
LaVergne TN
LVHW020044110826
845155LV00029B/632